What Baptists Believe

WHAT BAPTISTS BELIEVE

Herschel H. Hobbs

BROADMAN PRESS · Nashville, Tennessee

ISBN: 0–8054–8101–X
4281–01

DEWEY DECIMAL CLASSIFICATION: 230.6
Library of Congress catalog card number: 64–12411
Printed in the United States of America

To

*the Baptist editors
who render such a vital service in the
Lord's work and through whose co-operation
these articles were originally published*

Preface

Basic in the principles of Baptists is the concept of the competency of each individual soul before God. This involves the "priesthood of believers" whereby every believer may read and interpret the Scriptures as he is led by the Holy Spirit. This truth within itself asserts that the contents of this volume are in no sense an *official* statement of "what Baptists believe." They are the efforts of one Baptist to set forth what he believes that the Scriptures teach about certain elements of the Christian faith.

Nor does the author claim to present in these pages an exhaustive study of doctrine with respect to either topics or contents. In each case he has sought to state succinctly the meaning involved in certain selected elements of the faith. Related Scripture references are given to enable further study by those who desire to do so.

One of the most encouraging things about the current religious scene is a renewed interest in doctrine. It is one thing to believe. It is quite another thing to know what and why one believes. To say that one believes the Bible, and yet not know what it teaches, can hardly suffice in an age of critical analysis.

For this reason the author was delighted when the editor of one of the Baptist state papers requested that he write a weekly column under the caption, "Baptist Beliefs." At this editor's suggestion this column was offered to all Southern Baptist editors of state papers. Forthcoming requests from most of these editors were most gratifying. In addition, requests were received from other Baptist publications, including *The Australian Baptist* and some publications in languages other than the English tongue. The author is grateful to these editors for their co-operation in this labor of love. He is further indebted to Broadman Press for its request that these articles be offered for publication in this present volume.

If this edition serves in any way to extend this ministry, the author will be grateful beyond measure. If it helps to strengthen even one reader in the faith and to stimulate him to further study in showing himself "approved unto God, a workman that needeth not to be ashamed, rightly dividing the word of truth" (2 Tim. 2:15), its purpose will be realized to the glory of God.

Sources frequently referred to in this work include the following: E. Y. Mullins, *The Christian Religion in Its Doctrinal Expression;* A. T. Robertson, *Word Pictures in the New Testament;* J. H. Thayer, *A Greek-English Lexicon of the New Testament;* Alexander Maclaren, *The Gospel According to St. Matthew;* Herschel H. Hobbs, *Fundamentals of Our Faith;* H. F. Stevenson, *Titles of the Triune God;* B. H. Carroll, *An Interpretation of the English Bible.*

HERSCHEL H. HOBBS

Contents

1 GOD THE FATHER   13

Trinity; sovereignty of God; fatherhood of God; love of God; wrath of God; mercy and grace of God; will of God; foreknowledge of God; providence of God

2 JESUS CHRIST   28

Messiah or Christ; incarnation; virgin birth; Jesus' divine nature; Jesus' human nature; Son of man; self-emptying of Christ; Suffering Servant; vicarious death; bodily resurrection; ascension; postascension Christ; mediator; lordship of Christ

3 GOD THE HOLY SPIRIT   50

Speaking in tongues; interpretation of tongues; divine healing; prophecy; discerning of spirits; miracles

4 THE BIBLE   61

Revelation; inspiration; illumination

5 MAN   66

Free will of man; sin; unpardonable sin; priesthood of believers; prayer

CONTENTS

6 NEW TESTAMENT CHURCH   74

Foundation of the church; nature of the church; authority of the church; unity of the church; purpose of the church; baptism; Lord's Supper; pastor; deacons; missions

7 SALVATION   90

Atonement; conviction; repentance; confession; faith, conversion or regeneration; righteousness; sanctification; perseverance; glorification; election or predestination

8 LAST THINGS   108

Death; resurrection; second coming of Christ; millennium; judgment; heaven; hell; kingdom

9 MISCELLANY   119

Civil government; Christian citizenship; separation of church and state; religious liberty; angels; Satan; virgin Mary

What Baptists Believe

1
God the Father

The Bible does not seek to prove the existence of God. It declares him (Gen. 1:1). Belief in God, or a divine Being, is practically universal. The Bible dismisses the atheist with one terse verse. "The fool [unthinking person] hath said in his heart, There is no God" (Psalm 53:1). Note that he says it in his heart, the seat of his will. In his mind he knows better. But knowing it, he wishes that there was no God.

E. Y. Mullins gives us a definition of God. "God is the supreme personal Spirit; perfect in all his attributes; who is the source, support, and end of the universe; who guides it according to the wise, righteous, and loving purpose revealed in Jesus Christ; who indwells in all things by his Holy Spirit, seeking ever to transform them according to his own will and bring them to the goal of his kingdom."

There are three basic names for deity in the Old Testament: God (*Elohim*, Gen. 1:1); Lord (*Adonai*, Josh. 7:10); Jehovah (*Yahweh*, Lord in KJV, Gen. 2:4). The first (2,550 times in O.T.) is a plural of majesty and power. The second (340 times in O.T.) is a term of personal relationship and is used often as a cognate of Jehovah. The third (6,823 times in O.T.) defines the God of Israel as the true God and as Redeemer (cf.

Ex. 3:14; Isa. 42:8). In the New Testament, *Theos* corresponds to *Elohim;* Lord corresponds to *Jehovah;* Jesus means "Jehovah is salvation."

God is one Person (Deut. 6:4) who reveals himself in three manifestations as Father, Son, and Holy Spirit. He is a personal Spirit (John 4:24). He has no material body, except in his incarnation in Jesus Christ, nor is he limited by or to matter.

Systematic theology speaks of the attributes of God, which are usually divided into seven natural and four moral qualities relating to God's person. The natural attributes are his *self-existence* (from no source outside himself); *immutability* (unchanging character, nature, and purpose); *omnipresence* (present in all space and time); *immensity* (not confined to space or its laws); *eternity* (past, present, and future equally known to him; he inhabits eternity, Isa. 57:15); *omniscience* (God knows everything simultaneously); *omnipotence* (unlimited power in keeping with his nature, character, and purpose). God's moral attributes are *holiness* (supreme moral excellence or the sum of his other moral qualities); *righteousness* (self-affirmation of the right as opposed to the wrong); *truth* ("source and ground of all forms of knowing, and all objects of knowledge," Mullins); *love* (self-imparting nature of God seeking the highest good and complete possession of his creatures). Love is the attribute which envelops all others.

To conceive of God with respect to any one of his attributes apart from the others is to have only a partial picture of God. He reveals himself fully in and through Jesus Christ, who is interpreted to us by his Word and through his Holy Spirit.

Trinity

The word "trinity" is not found in the Bible. It was first used in the second century A.D. by Tertullian to express the truth taught in the Scriptures. It denotes the triune (three in one) revelation of God as Father (Gen. 1:1; Matt. 6:9), Son (John 8:36), and Holy Spirit (Gen. 1:2; John 14:26).

This does not mean that we worship three Gods. The natural mind of man, attempting to express the concept of the manifold nature of God, turned to idols (Rom. 1). God revealed himself as one God existing in three manifestations. He always has been Father, Son, and Spirit. Thus God the Son existed before Jesus was born. Jesus *is* the Son of God (John 3:16); through faith we may *become* sons of God (John 1:12). Jesus is God's begotten Son; we can become his adopted sons. As Holy Spirit, God indwells his children.

An examination of the Scriptures reveals that God is present in his triune revelation in his activity in creation (Gen. 1:1–2; Psalm 104:28–30; John 1:1–3; Col. 1:15–16), revelation (2 Tim. 3:6; Heb. 1:1–2; 2 Peter 1:21), redemption (Heb. 10:5–15), and providence (Matt. 6:25–31; John 14:1–3,16–18; 16:13). This is best seen in redemption. The Father proposed it; the Son provided it; the Holy Spirit propagates it (Heb. 10:5–15; 2 Cor. 5:19; Heb. 9:14). All three persons of God were present at the baptism of Jesus (Matt. 3:16–17: note voice [Father]; Jesus [Son]; dove [Holy Spirit]) and in his resurrection (Rom. 1:4).

Think of history as a stage. In the Old Testament God the Father is on stage, with the Son and Holy Spirit in the wings. In the Gospels God the Son is on stage, with the Father and Holy Spirit in the wings. Thereafter, God the Holy Spirit is on stage, with the Father and Son in the wings. All three Persons are present at all times, with each being the more prominent revelation at given stages of history. It is a mystery beyond our comprehension, but it is a fact.

This triune revelation is given for man's finite understanding. Paul pictures the concept of God in eternity (1 Cor. 15:24–28). In a redeemed and subjected universe the Father, Son, and Spirit reign supreme. There will still be Father, Son, and Spirit. But with our finite minds released from the limitations of the flesh, we shall know as we are known (1 Cor. 13:12). God (Father, Son, and Spirit) will be all in all (1 Cor. 15:28). For we shall see him as he is (1 John 3:2).

Sovereignty of God

The sovereignty of God means that God is sovereign or bears the rule in his universe (Psalm 10:16; Jer. 10:10). This relates to both nature and man. In the New Testament the word "kingdom" may well be rendered "sovereignty" (cf. Rev. 11:15). Satan claims world sovereignty (Matt. 4:8 ff.). In Christ God asserted his sovereignty in history (Matt. 4:17). It will be realized fully through his redemptive work (1 Cor. 15:24 ff.).

In the abstract sense God's sovereignty could mean that God, being all-powerful, may act as he wishes without regard to any other being or the attributes of his nature (Matt. 20:1–16). But in the concrete sense it means that he can do as he wills, said will being in accord with his nature which involves such attributes as his truth, holiness, righteousness, and love.

In this sense God has placed certain limitations on himself. He has willed not to violate the free will of man (Gen. 3). He does not act contrary to his own nature (Gen. 18:25). Thus God cannot regard evil as good. He cannot ignore sin. He cannot deny his love. He cannot lie or make two plus two equal five. The self-imposed limitations are not an evidence of God's weakness but of his omnipotence.

As sovereign, God chooses to work according to laws of his own making (Gen. 1:24–25; 8:22; Rom. 6:23). These laws are beneficent in purpose and become punitive only when violated. But God is not a prisoner within his laws. He acts supernaturally (miracle) when necessary to accomplish his moral and spiritual ends. Even here God does not act by caprice but according to higher laws unknown to man.

To the finite mind it is impossible to harmonize the sovereignty of God and the free will of man. But in the infinite mind of God there is no conflict. Finite minds can only accept both as facts in experience. The sovereignty of God never violates man's freedom. But it does require responsibility in man's choices.

The sovereignty of God is dedicated to the accomplishment of his spiritual purpose in history. "He keeps the reins of government in his hands. He guides the universe to his own glorious end. That end embodies the highest ideals of holiness and love" (Mullins; cf. Isa. 54:8; 55:1–9; Jer. 31:3; 1 Cor. 15:24–27; Eph. 3:1–11; Rev. 11:15).

Fatherhood of God

The revelation of God as the Father is uniquely that of Jesus. In the Old Testament there are allusions to God as Father (Job 1:6; Hos. 11:1). In the New Testament the fatherly nature of God toward all men is seen in such passages as Matthew 5:45; Luke 15:11–32; and Acts 17:28. But the distinct teaching of the New Testament is that God is "the Father" only in a spiritual relationship (John 4:23). Outside of Christ men are called "tares" or "children of the wicked one"; the "good seed" are "the children of the kingdom" (Matt. 13:38). The Pharisees were "of your father the devil" (John 8:44). But Jesus taught his disciples to pray to God as "Our Father . . . " (Matt. 6:8–9). In the New Testament the word "Father" is used of God 267 times. It is so used 122 times in John.

The relationship between the first and second persons of the Trinity is that of Father and Son. But their unity is seen in Jesus' words, "I and my Father are one" (John 10:30). The New Testament teaches that Jesus is the Son of God, and that men may become the sons of God.

How do men become sons of God? Universalism claims that

all men are sons of God and need only to claim their sonship. But this is to generalize the biblical teaching. The fact is that God is eternally Father in his nature. Men are constituted with the capacity to become sons of God not by their power but by God's grace. God desires all men to become such. But it is possible only by a change of nature described as being "born again" (John 3:3). This is made possible only by grace through faith (Eph. 2:8–10). "But as many as received him, to them gave he power [right, privilege] to become the sons of God, even to them that believe on his name" (John 1:12). Power means "out of being." So in such an experience God imparts his nature or being to those who receive his Son. Only these may be called "sons of God" in the true, spiritual sense. They become "children, then heirs; heirs of God, and joint-heirs with Christ" (Rom. 8:17). God is the Creator of all men, but he is "the Father" only to those who have become "sons" through faith in the Son.

As Father, God loves his children and gives good gifts to them (Matt. 7:11). He also disciplines his children in love (Heb. 12:6 ff.). The children of God are to live so that through them men will glorify their Heavenly Father (Matt. 5:16).

Love of God

"God is love" (1 John 4:8). Thus love is grounded in the very nature of God. E. Y. Mullins defines this love as "the self-imparting quality in the divine nature which leads God to seek the highest good and the most complete possession of his creatures."

Three principal words in the New Testament are rendered "love" (*phileō*, verb, 25 times; *agapaō*, verb, 142 times; *agapē*, noun, 116 times). *Phileō* denotes friendliness prompted by sense and emotion. *Agapaō* (*agapē*) connotes a love grounded in admiration, veneration, and esteem (Thayer). At times the words appear to be used interchangeably (John 14:23, *agapaō*;

16:27, *phileō*), but the above distinction qualifies the meaning in either case. Perhaps their difference is best seen in John 21 where the play on each word is significant (vv. 15*a*, 16*a*, *agapaō;* vv. 15*b*, 16*b*, *phileō;* v. 17, three times, *phileō*). When Peter failed to come up to the higher love, Jesus descended to the lower or the love which Peter had. Hence Peter's grief. It is evident then that *agapaō* refers to a higher love than *phileō* does. The latter denotes a friendly, emotional love; the former is a love embodying absolute loyalty toward its object. The more numerous use of *agapaō* is indicative of the greater emphasis placed upon it in the New Testament.

In "God is love" (1 John 4:8), the word is *agapē*. It is a favorite word of John in both verb and noun form (*agapaō*, John, 37 times, 1 John, 28 times; *agapē*, John, 7 times, 1 John, 18 times). This love finds its source in God (1 John 4:10) and is man's response to God's love (1 John 4:19). It is the love which men in Christ should have for each other (1 John 4:11; note "charity" in 1 Cor. 13 is *agapē*). It is out of this love that God proposes salvation for men (John 3:16; Rom. 8:37), and that Christ acted to provide this salvation (Gal. 2:20; Eph. 5:2).

An analysis of this love in 1 John 4:8–21 is most revealing— God's love coming down to man (v. 10), man's love rising in response to God's love (v. 19), the Christian's love going out to other believers. Pause to visualize the directions in which this love moves. They form a cross, suggesting that this love finds its complete expression in the cross. The proof of our love for God is our love for our fellow Christians (v. 20).

Wrath of God

The wrath of God is not angry passion, vindictiveness, or hatred. It is his resistance to sin, which expresses itself in penalty. In essence this penalty is spiritual death or the separation of the soul from God.

Two New Testament words are rendered wrath with respect to God (*thumos* and *orgē*). The former denotes a reaction of boiling up and soon subsiding. The latter denotes that which rises gradually and becomes more settled or abiding. With one exception (Rom. 2:8), *thumos* appears only in Revelation (14:10,19; 15:1,7; 16:1) with reference to God's wrath. *Orgē* is the more general word for the wrath of God (cf. Matt. 3:7; John 3:36; Rom. 1:18; 2:5; Col. 3:6; Rev. 6:16 f.; 19:15). The two words appear together in Romans 2:8 where they are rendered "indignation and wrath" (*orgē kai thumos*). The gradual and abiding indignation bursts forth in boiling wrath or retribution (cf. Revelation).

The wrath of God (*orgē*) has been defined as the law of God in operation (cf. Rom. 1:18). God's laws are for man's good. When he defies them they go right on working, and man is broken on them. Compare the law of gravity and the "wages of sin." Thus, the wrath of God is not an emotion of God. Rather, it is his fixed resistance to rebellion against his law.

God has not appointed man to wrath (1 Thess. 5:9). We are children of wrath because of our sinful nature (Eph. 2:3; cf. John 3:36). Through Christ man may be saved from God's wrath (Rom. 5:9).

On the cross God poured out his wrath on Christ, not as a personal sinner, but as one who became sin for us (2 Cor. 5:21). Thus the sin-death principle operated in him as he completely identified himself with sinful man, not as a participant in sin, but as the sin bearer (John 1:29).

Over against the wrath of God (Rom. 1:18) the gospel declares the righteousness of God (Rom. 1:17), God's activity in Christ whereby he declares us righteous as though we had not sinned. This he does as we believe in Christ as Saviour (Rom. 1:16). Henceforth we abide, not under God's wrath, but in his mercy and grace (Eph. 2:1-7).

Mercy and Grace of God

The mercy of God is related to the love of God. God is love in his nature. He can never cease to be love. But he shows mercy as he wills (Luke 1:50). God loves the sinner whether he repents or not. But his mercy is conditioned on repentance. This does not mean that God gives mercy grudgingly. He is abundant in mercy (Eph. 2:4; 1 Peter 1:3), but in his righteousness he can show mercy only upon conditions of his own choosing. "Mercy is love expressing itself in forgiveness and remission of penalty from the guilty" (Mullins) who repent of their sins (Luke 18:13).

In the New Testament "mercy" renders a word (28 times in N.T., verb form 31 times) meaning "kindness or good will towards the miserable and afflicted, joined with a desire to relieve them" (Thayer). It is used of men toward men (Matt. 9:13; 12:7; James 2:13). More often it speaks of God's attitude toward men (Luke 1:50; 1 Tim. 1:2; Titus 1:4). Specifically it speaks of God's desire to give salvation through Christ (Luke 1:54; Rom. 15:9; Eph. 2:4-5). Twice it refers to the mercy that Christ will show to believers in the judgment (2 Tim. 1:18; Jude 21).

According to E. Y. Mullins, mercy alone does not show the fulness of God's love. This is seen in grace. "Mercy and grace are the negative and positive aspects of love toward the sinful. Mercy takes the bitter cup of penalty and pain from the hand of the guilty and empties it. Grace fills it to the brim with blessings. Mercy spares the object; grace claims it for its own. Mercy rescues from peril; grace imparts a new nature and bestows a new standing. Mercy is God's love devising a way of escape. Grace is the same love devising ways of transforming its object into the divine likeness and enabling it to share the divine blessedness."

The divine order in God's love to repentant sinners is "grace, mercy, and peace" (1 Tim. 1:2). And it is all through Christ.

"Grace" (Greek, *charis*) is one of the greatest words in human language. In classical Greek it sometimes means "sweetness, charm, or loveliness." It often referred to a favor done out of generosity (always to one's friends) with no thought of a return. In the New Testament "grace" in this sense refers to the generous act of God toward his enemies (Rom. 3:23-26; 5:1-10).

The word for "grace" (*charis*) appears 156 times in the New Testament. In the Gospels it is found only in Luke (8 times, translated once as "grace," 2:40) and John (1:14-17). It is a favorite word of Paul, appearing in his epistles 102 times.

The history of this word is most revealing: (1) to make a gift, (2) to forgive a debt, (3) to forgive a wrong, (4) to forgive sin. Basically, then, grace means a gift (cf. Rom. 3:24; 6:23; Eph. 2:8). In the sense of redemption, grace is the unmerited favor of God bestowed on the sinner through the merits of Christ (John 1:14,16-17). C. E. Autrey defines grace as "something which God does for a sinner that no one else or nothing else can do for him." In the New Testament "grace" is contrasted with "works" (Eph. 2:8-10). If salvation is by grace it cannot be by works in any sense, for this would be a negation of the meaning of grace. Regeneration is by grace alone. But God's grace uses the works of a Christian in producing the kind of Christian character which he designs for each believer.

The word "grace" is often used in greetings by New Testament writers to express the sum total of God's spiritual blessings (Rom. 1:7; 16:20; 1 Cor. 1:3; Gal. 1:3). "Grace" in this sense is sometimes used with "peace" (cf. Rom. 1:7; Eph. 1:2), combining the Greek and the Hebrew words of greeting. "Grace" is also used in the sense of monetary gifts (1 Cor. 16:3, liberality) or of abilities which are due to the grace of God (Eph. 4:7). A kindred word (*charisma*) is used in this latter sense only by Paul (Rom. 12:6; 1 Cor. 1:7; save one example in 1 Peter 4:10).

The term "falling from grace" is a misnomer. "Ye are fallen from grace" (Gal. 5:4) literally means "ye are fallen away from grace." The context clearly means "ye left the sphere of grace in Christ and took your stand in the sphere of law" (Robertson). In Hebrews 12:15 the sense of "grace" refers not to redemption but to the realization of all spiritual blessings or to realize the goal of one's Christian life (Thayer).

Will of God

The will of God is an expression of the life of God. God's life is expressed in his activity of thought, feeling, and will (Ezra 7:18; John 1:13; Rom. 12:2).

Two verbs are rendered in the New Testament for "willing." *Boulomai* refers to deliberate will or purpose (Mark 15:15; Acts 5:28,33). *Thelō* is related to resolve or purpose (Rom. 9:16). Thayer distinguishes between them by saying that the former seems to designate the will which follows deliberation, the latter the will which proceeds from inclination. Authorities are disagreed on the distinction, and at times they seem to be used interchangeably. But Thayer lists *thelēma* (noun of *thelō*) as referring to God's purpose to bless mankind through Christ (Acts 22:14; Eph. 1:9; Col. 1:9). It is also used to express that which God wishes for man to do (Rom. 12:2; Col. 4:12). The primary word used to refer to God's will is *thelō* and its derivatives (Matt. 6:10; 8:2; 9:13; 26:39; John 4:34).

The will of God may be regarded severally. His judicial will is his commandments (cf. Ex. 20). God's punitive will relates to the consequences of sin (Rom. 6:23). Distinction should be made between God's will as causing a thing or permitting it (Job 1:12; 2:6). Even in his permissive will God sets limits beyond which such shall not be done. This explains much of the tragedy of life. God does not cause such, but on occasion he permits it in that he does not perform a miracle to prevent it. Many such events occur when we violate God's will, not because he wills them (Luke 19:41 ff.; cf. Ex. 8:15).

The will of God may be regarded as intentional, circumstantial, and ultimate. God intends only good for man (Gen. 1:27–28; 2:15–17). But circumstances arise which bring the opposite result (Gen. 3; Job 1–2; 2 Cor. 12:7 ff.). In such God wills that we shall so conduct ourselves as to glorify him. And he sustains us in them (2 Cor. 12:9). God's ultimate will is that God's intentional will ultimately shall be done (Job 42:10 ff.; cf. Gen. 3:15; John 3:16; Rom. 8:28).

The will of God the Father and God the Son were/are one (John 4:34; cf. Matt. 26:42). Jesus taught us to pray, "Thy will be done in earth, as it is in heaven" (Matt. 6:10). The will of God may not always be easy, but it is always right. George W. Truett was fond of saying that to know the will of God is the greatest knowledge, and to do the will of God is the greatest achievement.

Foreknowledge of God

The foreknowledge of God is based upon his omniscience or all knowledge. Since the Bible views God as present at all times and all places contemporaneously in his universe, he knows all things simultaneously. Thus he foreknows all things before they occur.

The Greek verb "foreknow" (*proginōsko*) occurs five times in the New Testament where it is variously translated (Acts 26:5, know; Rom. 8:29; 11:2, foreknow; 1 Peter 1:20, foreordain; 2 Pet. 3:17, know before). The noun "foreknowledge" is used twice (Acts 2:23; 1 Peter 1:2).

There are three principal positions in theology with regard to this doctrine. Calvinists hold that since God has willed what will happen in the future, he knows that it will happen. Arminians insist that while man is free, God knows his choices in advance. Socinians contend that God knows all that is knowable, but that events determined by man's free choice are unknowable.

Two questions arise out of the first and third positions. First, does God's foreknowledge of an event predetermine its occurrence? The answer is "no." To foreknow an automobile accident does not cause it. God's foreknowledge of man's sin does not necessitate it. Or else it is not a matter of free choice, and it makes God the author of evil. God does not cause evil in any sense, nor does he will it. He permits it in that he does not intervene to prevent it. But to say that God wills it, therefore it must be, is to ignore the holy nature of God.

Second, does man's free choice rule out the foreknowledge of God? Those holding this view insist that foreknowledge is based upon a chain of antecedent events which determine the final result. That free choice is not determined by antecedent events, else it is not free choice. Therefore, God cannot foreknow the choice.

But God's omniscience is not serially obtained. "God knows immediately and directly without the need of inference from antecedent motives" (Mullins). Otherwise, God could not control and guide his universe to his purposeful ends. "Other wills, not his own, would fix the course of events and the destiny of his creatures" (Mullins). The Bible teaches that God does foreknow man's choices (cf. Job 1:8 ff.).

The New Testament uses of foreknowledge relate it to both sin and salvation. Foreknowing man's sin God had a foreknowledge of the cross (Acts 2:23). But his foreknowledge did not itself cause them. Because he foreknew sin, he also foreknew the cross, his remedy for sin. Foreknowledge is also related to election (1 Peter 1:2). This refers to the election of individuals only in the sense that God foreknew who would receive or reject his provision for sin (cf. Rom. 8:29a). But even God's foreknowledge leaves man free and responsible in his choice.

The Bible does not try to harmonize God's sovereignty and man's free will with respect to his foreknowledge. It assumes them both to be true. This is a mystery to our finite minds but not to the infinite mind of an omniscient God.

Providence of God

The word "providence" appears only once in the Scriptures (Acts 24:2, KJV), and that is in reference to a political ruler. But the word is suggestive of the broader and more extensive providence of God.

This English word is derived from the Latin *pro* (forward) and *videre* (to see), hence provide. Thus it means to see forward or ahead. Note the word "provision," supplying in advance, especially food. The word "providence" may be understood as "provide-ence."

The Greek word rendered "providence" is *pronoia*, forethought (Acts 24:2). Its verb form is *pronoeō*, to know or think beforehand (Rom. 12:17; 2 Cor. 8:21; 1 Tim. 5:8).

E. Y. Mullins defines the providence of God as "his control or direction of the universe toward the end which he has chosen." It involves the creation (Gen. 1:1,27) and care of both the natural universe and man as God guides both to his spiritual ends.

Thus God's providence is related to his divine purpose in his control of the universe (Eph. 3:11). It involves God's sovereignty as expressed in the physical (Gen. 1:3–31) and moral laws of the universe (Ex. 20:1 ff.). But it respects man's freedom, else God would be responsible for evil (Gen. 3:1 ff.). It speaks of both God's transcendence and immanence with respect to the universe. He is above nature and man. Yet he is concerned and involved in both. This presupposes both miracles and natural events (Mal. 3:11) in God's operation.

The providence of God encompasses the race (Matt. 5:45) as well as individuals (Matt. 6:25 ff.; 10:29–31). To accomplish his purpose God uses both nations (Isa. 45:1 ff.) and individuals (Gen. 12:1 ff.). This is especially seen in the nation Israel (Ex. 19:1 ff.) and in the church (1 Peter 2:9 ff.).

God's providence does not pre-empt the possibility of evil in nature and man. But he overrules the evil as he pursues his purpose (Rom. 8:28). The ultimate purpose of God is expressed in the redemption of the universe (2 Peter 3:13) and man (Eph. 3:9; 1 Tim. 2:4). But men are not saved as a race. Only those are saved who come to God through faith in Jesus Christ (John 3:16).

The providence of God envisions a redeemed universe (Rom. 8:19–23) and people (Rev. 5:9) wherein "God may be all in all" (1 Cor. 15:27–28).

2
Jesus Christ

Jesus Christ is the key to our knowledge of God and of history. "Jesus" is the Greek equivalent of the Hebrew word "Joshua" or "Yeshua," meaning "Jehovah is salvation." It is our Lord's human and personal name, signifying that in him Jehovah reveals himself in salvation (cf. Acts 4:12). "Christ" is our Lord's official title. It is the Greek synonym for the Hebrew "Messiah," meaning the Anointed One. When "Lord" is used relating to Jesus Christ, it is the equivalent of "Jehovah." The term "Son of God" is used repeatedly in the New Testament with reference to Jesus. Under oath Jesus testified that he is the Son of God (Matt. 26:63–64). Thomas called him God (John 20:28) with no protest from Jesus. His favorite title for himself was "Son of man," suggesting his identity with man.

Jesus is the incarnation (in flesh) of God the Son, the second Person of the Trinity (John 1:1–14). As such he is coexistent, coequal, and coeternal with God the Father (vv. 1–2). He is the Creator of the universe and the Source of life (vv. 3–4). He is the "image [exact manifestation] of the invisible God" (Col. 1:15). He is the Source, immediate Agent, and Goal of the universe, both material and spiritual (v. 16). He is the Head of the church and the Reconciler of man with God (vv. 18–22). He is God become flesh (John 1:14). He is the God-man. This involves his virgin birth (Matt. 1:22–23), sinless life (Heb. 4:15), vicarious death (John 10:17; 11:50), bodily resurrection (Rom. 1:4; 1 Cor. 15:3–5), ascension (Acts 1:9), continuing intercession (Heb. 7:25), and second coming (1 Thess. 4:16). He is now reigning in his mediatorial kingdom (1 Cor. 15:25). Ultimately he shall be "King of Kings, and Lord of Lords" (Rev. 19:16).

Probably the greatest single verse declaring the deity of Jesus Christ is Colossians 2:9. Literally it reads, "For in him alone is continuously and permanently at home all the full essence of divine powers and attributes, the state of being God, in bodily form."

Messiah or Christ

"Messiah" is a Hebrew word (*mashiach*) meaning "smeared" or "anointed." As an official title it appears in the Hebrew form only twice in the Old Testament (Dan. 9:25–26) and twice in the New Testament (John 1:41; 4:25). But the idea of "anointing" is abundantly found in the Old Testament.

Anointing with olive oil, sometimes perfumed, was a part of the daily toilet of the Hebrews. However, among the poor it was probably used only on special occasions (Ruth 3:3). During a time of mourning one abstained from this practice (2 Sam. 14:2; cf. 2 Sam. 12:20). Anointing a guest with oil was an act of hospitality (Psalm 23:5; cf. Luke 7:46).

In the religious sense anointing applied to both things and persons. Stones might be anointed to constitute altars (Gen. 28:18–20; cf. 31:13). Also the tabernacle (Ex. 40:9), its altar (Ex. 40:10), and its vessels (Ex. 40:11; Lev. 8:11) were thus consecrated. As "anointed" they were holy unto Jehovah (Lev. 8:10).

Persons set apart for Jehovah's service also were anointed. This practice probably originated in Egypt, and was practiced by the Canaanites prior to the Hebrew invasion. Among the Hebrews this custom applied to priests (Ex. 30:30), kings (1 Sam. 10:1; 15:1; 16:12; 2 Sam. 2:4; note Elijah's anointing a pagan king, 1 Kings 19:15-16), and prophets (1 Kings 19:16, only example but see Isa. 61:1). To anoint one with sacred oil was to impart to the anointed a special endowment of the Spirit of Jehovah (1 Sam. 16:13; cf. Isa. 61:1). Hence the sacred regard for the "Lord's anointed" (1 Sam. 26:23).

The word "Messiah" came to be applied to One who would be sent from Jehovah (cf. Dan. 9:25-26). He would be Prophet, Priest, and King "anointed" of God by his Spirit (Isa. 61:1; cf. Acts 10:38). Unfortunately, however, the priestly, sacrificial role of the Messiah was lost in the Jewish concept. The role of the prophet survived but dimly (Matt. 16:14). In their worldly, political ambitions the Jews came to look for a political, military Messiah (cf. John 6:15; cf. 6:26,60 ff.) who would deliver them from Roman bondage and set up an earthly kingdom (cf. Luke 24:21; Acts 1:6). This picture abounds in the Jewish writings between the Old and New Testaments. Hence Satan's proposal to Jesus (Matt. 4:8-10). For this reason, "He came unto his own [things], and his own [people] received him not [did not welcome him]" (John 1:11). But a remnant did receive him (cf. Luke 2:26).

The Greek word "Christ" is the equivalent of the Hebrew word "Messiah" (anointed) and is used in the Greek translation of the Old Testament (Septuagint) to translate the Hebrew word. It is used of the king of Israel (1 Sam. 2:10) and of Cyrus, king of Persia (Isa. 45:1). The proper name "Christ" (*ho Christos*) is not found in the Greek Old Testament but is first used in the apocryphal book of Enoch (48:10; 52:4; Thayer). However, the messianic idea itself is present in the Old Testament (cf. Psalm 2:2, Thayer). In the New Testament the term "Christ" embodied all of the Jewish expectations of "the coming One" (Luke 7:19).

It is significant that Jesus never used the term "Christ" to refer to himself, due doubtless to the revolutionary, political connotation attached to the title by the Jews. But when the Samaritan woman spoke of "Messias," Jesus said, "I that speak unto thee am he" (John 4:25–26). He commended Peter for so declaring him (Matt. 16:16–17), adding that upon himself, the Christ, he would build his church (Matt. 16:18). At his trial, under oath, he admitted to being the Christ (Matt. 26:63–64). However, Jesus repeatedly referred to himself as "the Son of man" (cf. Matt. 8:20; 12:40; Mark 10:45; Luke 19:10), a title which carried messianic connotations (John 12:34). Jesus' followers definitely regarded him as "the Christ" (Matt. 16:16; cf. Acts 2:36; 17:3).

The New Testament presents a progression in the significance of the term "Christ." In the beginning it was an official title or the title of an office. Jesus was "the Christ" (Matt. 2:4; Luke 2:26). But it came to be used as a personal name, "Christ" (cf. 1 Cor. 15:3 ff.), yet still with the significance of "Messiah." In this sense it carried both the historical and eternal aspects of the Saviour's work. At times it was combined with the names "Jesus" and "Lord" (cf. Rom. 5:11; 6:23; 8:2). In such combinations were emphasized the eternal aspect or deity (Christ), the Saviourhood (Jesus), and the Lordship (Lord, Jehovah). The order in which these words were used varied the particular emphasis of the moment in a given combination.

"As His human name [Jesus] assures us that our God is our Saviour, so His divine name [Christ] declares that our Saviour is our God" (Stevenson).

Incarnation

The word "incarnation" does not appear in the Bible, but the idea is present throughout the New Testament. Incarnation means that God in Jesus Christ revealed himself to man in a flesh and blood body (1 Tim. 3:16). Thus God who is Spirit (John 4:24) manifested himself to the natural senses of man (1 John 1:1–3).

This idea was a major issue in first-century Christology as it is today. Gnostic philosophers denied the incarnation. The Docetic Gnostics said that Jesus only seemed (*dokeō*, seem) to have a flesh and blood body. The Cerinthian Gnostics (from their leader, Cerinthus) said that Christ or deity came upon Jesus at his baptism (cf. Matt. 3:16–17) and left him on the cross (cf. Matt. 27:46). Thus, said they, Christ neither was born nor did he die. Many New Testament passages reflect conflict with these ideas.

John says that "the Word [Christ] was made [became] flesh, and dwelt among us" (John 1:14; cf. 1:1). It is commonly and correctly said that Jesus was God. More to the point, God was or became Jesus. This suggests the dual idea of the deity-humanity of Jesus. In his person God completely identified himself with man apart from sin.

As human, Jesus grew tired (Mark 4:38; John 4:6), became hungry (Matt. 4:2), thirsty (John 19:28); he died and was buried. He knew emotion: wonder (Mark 6:6), compassion (Luke 7:13), and joy (Luke 10:21). He was tempted (Matt. 4:1–11) yet without sin.

As God he forgave sin (Matt. 9:2–6), assumed judgeship (Matt. 25:31 ff.), revealed God's will (Matt. 11:27), arose from the dead (Luke 24:1–8; Rom. 1:4), and commissioned his church (Matt. 28:18–20). He claimed identity with the Father (John 14:8–11). Paul sums it up when he declares that "God was in Christ, reconciling the world unto himself" (2 Cor. 5:19). This truth is repeatedly avowed—that God in Jesus manifested himself in the flesh to accomplish the salvation of man (Eph. 2:15; Col. 1:22; Heb. 4:15; 1 Peter 3:18; 4:1). John related orthodoxy to one's recognition that Christ came in the flesh (1 John 4:2–3; 2 John 7; cf. Gnostic heresy).

The truth of the incarnation involves the fact of the virgin birth (Luke 1:26 ff.). The incarnation of God in Christ is emphatically declared in Colossians 2:9.

Virgin Birth

The virgin birth of Jesus, along with his crucifixion and resurrection, forms the triumvirate of salvation. Apart from the virgin birth, the crucifixion is a tragedy, the resurrection is unthinkable, and the entire gospel is assailable. But admit the virgin birth and the remainder of the gospel is reasonable indeed. The virgin birth is one of the most completely authenticated facts in ancient history.

The Bible clearly teaches the virgin birth of Jesus. It is anticipated in Genesis (3:15), prophesied in Isaiah (7:14), and proclaimed in Matthew and Luke. In Isaiah 7:14 the Hebrew word *almah* means a young, unmarried woman and, therefore, a virgin. Matthew 1:23 clearly cites the virgin birth of Jesus as the fulfilment of Isaiah 7:14. Mark does not relate the birth of Jesus at all. His account begins with Jesus' public ministry. John omits direct reference to it as already recounted but implies it in 1:14. Paul allows for the virgin birth in Galatians 4:4. To deny the virgin birth because these do not specifically relate it is to argue from silence. Mark, John, and Paul all present Jesus as the Son of God.

Until the rise of modern liberalism there was no question posed about the virgin birth except by those who were prejudiced against the deity of Christ and ignorant of the facts concerning his origin (cf. Matt. 13:55; John 6:42; 8:41; the Gnostics). Modern denials of the virgin birth are based on so-called rationalistic, scientific, and historical grounds. Matthew Arnold brushed it aside by saying, "I do not believe in the virgin birth of Christ because it involves a miracle, and miracles do not happen." This statement is neither reason, science, nor history.

Is the virgin birth reasonable? How else could God invade history for redemption? How else could Jesus be the sinless Son of God? If Jesus be not virgin born, he is just a man and not the divine Saviour.

Is the virgin birth scientific? Does science know all of God's laws? Admittedly the virgin birth is a miracle. It is God working according to his laws unknown to man to accomplish his spiritual purpose. If God can create human life by natural law, can he not create divine-human life by spiritual law?

Is the virgin birth historical? The Gospels are credible historical records. Luke, a scientist-historian, relates the virgin birth, and he has never been discredited as to historical accuracy.

The virgin birth declares Jesus to be the Son of God (Matt. 1:23; Luke 1:35; John 1:14). It speaks of his sinless nature (John 8:46). It gives the promise of our new birth by the power of the Holy Spirit (cf. Luke 1:35; John 3:5–6).

Those who deny the virgin birth affirm Jesus' sinless life. Bruce says, "A sinless man is as much a miracle in the moral world as a Virgin Birth is a miracle in the physical world."

Strange to say, the first question as to the virgin birth was raised by the virgin Mary herself (Luke 1:34). God's answer to her is his answer to all. "For with God nothing shall be impossible" (Luke 1:37).

Jesus' Divine Nature

The New Testament reveals the nature of Jesus as both divine and human. This divine-human nature is incomprehensible (Rom. 11:33; 16:25–27), but it is real nevertheless.

As divine, Jesus is the Christ, the eternal Son of God (John 1:1–2; 8:58; 17:5). He is the Creator of the universe (John 1:3–4; Heb. 1:2). He is the Sphere (by, *en*, in the sphere of, Col. 1:16) in which creation took place, the immediate

Agent (by, *dia*, through, 1:16) in creation, and the Goal (for, *eis*, unto, 1:16) of creation. He is the center of the universe (Col. 1:17, consist, hold together). He is the Lord of all creation (cf. firstborn and before, Col. 1:15,17). He is the image (personal manifestation) of the living God (Col. 1:15) and the "express image" (exact manifestation, Heb. 1:3) of his person. Literally, Paul says, "For in him and him alone is permanently and abidingly at home all the very essence of deity, the state of being God in bodily form" (Col. 2:9).

As the eternal Son of God, he is "the Lamb slain from the foundation of the world" (Rev. 13:8; cf. John 1:29; Heb. 10:5–7). Yet, he became flesh and dwelt among us (John 1:14). In his birth he was conceived of the Holy Spirit and born of the virgin Mary (Matt. 1:18–23; cf. Isa. 7:14). Thus he possessed no sinful nature (John 8:46; Rom. 5:12–21). He perfectly fulfilled the law of God (John 4:34; Rom. 10:4). He was declared of God to be his Son (Matt. 3:17; 17:5).

Jesus' disciples recognized him as "the Christ, the Son of the living God" (Matt. 16:16; John 11:27; cf. Mark 1:23–24). In his transfiguration (Matt. 17:2) the wick of his deity which had been turned low was suddenly turned up to a glorious brightness.

Some insist that Jesus never claimed deity for himself. But note John 3:16,18; 5:25 ff. He repeatedly claimed to be one with God (John 8:54; 10:18,36–37; 14:6–13; 16:28; 17:21,24). He performed the works of God (Mark 2:5–12; John 5:17; 10:25; 11:43–44; 17:4). Without protest he allowed others so to declare him (Matt. 14:33; John 1:49). Under oath he admitted that he was the Son of God (Matt. 26:63–64; v. 64, "Thou hast said" in the Greek is such an admission; cf. 27:43).

So Jesus died as the Son of God (Luke 23:46; cf. Matt. 27:54). His resurrection proved his deity (Matt. 12:38–40; Rom. 1:4; cf. Acts 2:23–24; 3:14–15; Phil. 2:5–11). Thus "God was in Christ, reconciling the world unto himself" (2 Cor. 5:19).

With Thomas we can say, "My Lord and my God" (John 20:28).

Jesus' Human Nature

Many who acclaim the deity of Jesus Christ forget his humanity. It is as great an error to deny the latter as to deny the former. For Jesus is the God-man.

In his incarnation Jesus completely identified himself with man apart from sin. The Word became flesh (John 1:14). Born of a virgin, he entered the world as a baby (Matt. 1:18 ff.; Luke 1:31; 2:7; Gal. 4:4). As a child he grew in body, mind, and spirit (Luke 2:40–52). As a man he grew tired (Mark 4:38), knew hunger (Matt. 4:2) and thirst (John 19:28), experienced wonder (Matt. 8:10, "marvelled" is "wondered"), and expressed a limitation of knowledge (Matt. 24:36; Acts 1:7).

In his humanity Jesus "was in all points tempted like as we are, yet without sin" (Heb. 4:15; cf. Matt. 4:1–11). Luke says that Satan tempted him with "every kind of temptation" (4:13, literal meaning).

Could Jesus have yielded to temptation? Yes. Or else his temptations were not real. If not, then he merely pretended to be tempted. To say that he could not yield to temptation is to make him guilty of the sin of hypocrisy, a sin which he vehemently condemned. The truth is that in his humanity he had the power to sin, but he also had the power not to sin. He endured the fires of temptation but was not overcome thereby. Thus we have a High Priest who was touched with our infirmities yet without sin. Therefore, he is able to help us when we are tempted (Heb. 4:15–16).

Despite his temptations Jesus was sinless (Matt. 27:4,24; Luke 23:14; John 8:46). Though he knew no sin, yet he was made sin for us, that we might be made the righteousness of God in him (2 Cor. 5:21).

God in Jesus Christ lived as a flesh and blood man (2 Cor. 5:19; cf. John 1:14). He died as flesh and blood (Matt. 27:35 ff.; John 19:34; Heb. 5:7; 9:12; 1 Peter 1:18–19; Rev. 5:9,12). He was raised bodily from the grave and appeared to his disciples (Matt. 28:9–10,16 ff.; Luke 24:13 ff.; John 20:14 to 21:23; 1 Cor. 15:4–8). When he ascended to the Father he did so as the God-man (Acts 1:9–11; Heb. 9:12,24–28). Thus, he is forever God and forever man (Rev. 1:18).

In the first century there arose a philosophy called gnosticism. It denied the union of God and man in the person of Jesus. One group (Docetics, from Greek word *dokeō*, I seem) said that Jesus did not have a flesh and blood body; he only *seemed* to have one. Another group (Cerinthians, from their leader, Cerinthus) said that Christ came upon Jesus at his baptism (Matt. 3:16–17) and left him on the cross (Matt. 27:46). Much of the New Testament reflects its opposition to these errors (cf. John 1:14; 19:34; Col. 1:13–20; 2:9; 1 John 1:1–3; 2:22; 5:1; 2 John 7).

In one form or another these ancient errors continue even today. But the Bible still declares Jesus Christ to be Son of God and Son of man. And the Christian experience affirms its message.

Son of Man

The title "Son of man" was the favorite self-designation of Jesus. It appears eighty-seven times in the New Testament. And with four exceptions (John 12:34; Acts 7:56; Rev. 1:13; 14:14), it is used only by Jesus. Apparently he preferred this title to Christ and Son of David (used by Jesus only once by inference, Mark 12:35; Luke 20:41), since to the Jews these latter names carried a political meaning.

The phrase "Son of man" occurs repeatedly throughout the Old Testament (ninety times in Ezekiel). However, with one exception (Dan. 7:13), it has reference to men only. Its use by

Jesus probably came from Daniel 7:13. Here, after the fall of successive world empires, there appeared one "like the Son of man" to receive his kingdom, which was quite unlike the earthly empires. Note that "Son of man" does not appear in the New Testament after the Gospels, except in Acts 7:56, until Revelation 1:13 where Christ appears as dwelling in his churches (cf. 14:14).

"Son of man" suggests Jesus' identity with man for man's redemption. It connotes our Lord's voluntary entrance into humanity as representative man, "the last Adam" (1 Cor. 15:45), to accomplish man's salvation. Thus Jesus used it with reference to his earthly ministry (Matt. 8:20; Luke 19:10), his death and resurrection (Matt. 12:40; 17:9; 22–23), and his second coming (Matt. 13:41; 24:27; Luke 21:36). While the Gospels picture Jesus as "Son of man," they leave no doubt but that he is more than man. He is the God-man: perfect in deity and in humanity.

In his heavenly glory he still bears his relation to man. He is "the Son of man" (Acts 7:56) and "like unto the Son of man" (Rev. 1:13; 14:14). "When the Son of man shall come in his glory" (Matt. 25:31), his own will be "changed" (1 Cor. 15:52). Therefore, "Beloved, now are we the sons of God, and it doth not yet appear what we shall be: but we know that, when he shall appear, we shall be like him; for we shall see him as he is" (1 John 3:2).

Our Lord became the "Son of man" that we might become "sons of God" (cf. John 1:12).

Self-emptying of Christ

This truth is found in Philippians 2:5–11. In theology it is known as *kenosis* (from *kenos*, empty). It expresses that which transpired when Christ became man.

Of what did Christ empty himself? Some say that he ceased to be divine. Others say that he emptied himself of his omnipotence (all power), omniscience (all wisdom), and omnipresence (all presence), but that he retained his holiness and love. Both views are in error. Actually he emptied himself from the "form" of God into the "form" of man (Phil. 2:6–7). The figure is that of, say, pouring water from a round glass into a square glass. No water is lost. It simply changes its outward appearance. Thus, the incarnation of God in human form was divine omnipotence, omniscience, and love devising and performing God's saving act for lost men.

Obviously this self-emptying involved self-limitation. Christ retained his divine qualities and powers but brought them under the restraints of human life. Lightfoot says that "He stripped himself of the insignia of majesty" to take on himself the form of a slave. A. T. Robertson says that he "gave up his environment of glory. He took upon himself limitations of place (space) and of knowledge and of power, though still on earth retaining more of these than any mere man." None of these self-limitations produced errors of knowledge or conduct, for he was sinless (Heb. 4:15.)

Paul says that because of this self-emptying God "highly exalted him" above and beyond (*huper*) the state of glory which was his before the incarnation (cf. John 17:5). In what sense? Jesus returned to heaven with his humanity as well as with his deity. Before the incarnation he was "Christ." Now he is "Jesus Christ." He is not only creator and Lord. In addition, he is now also Saviour (Jesus is "Jehovah is salvation") and Lord.

Thus "at the name of Jesus" the whole creation bows in submission and acknowledges him as "Lord" (cf. 1 Cor. 15:24 ff.). This does not mean universal salvation. Those who receive him do it willingly and joyfully in salvation. Those who reject him will one day be made by his power to admit, without salvation, that he is Lord although they rejected him as such.

Suffering Servant

Two views are commonly held with respect to the "Servant" passages in Old Testament prophecy (cf. Isaiah 42 ff. and others). One is that they refer to the nation Israel. In certain instances this is true (cf. Isa. 41:8–9; 44:1). But in other passages the references are to a person (Isa. 42:1 ff.; but note 42:19–20 where reference is to Judah). In each instance the context must be the deciding factor.

Some interpreters hold the national view regarding the "Suffering Servant" passages (cf. Isa. 52:13 to 53:12). However, a careful reading reveals the Servant to be a person, not a nation. Christian theology sees these as prophecies concerning the sufferings of Jesus Christ, hence the "Suffering Servant." There is no incident in Hebrew history to which this above mentioned passage might refer.

However, when it is studied in the light of the life, death, and resurrection of Jesus its meaning is quite clear. Isaiah 53:4–6 reads like an eyewitness account of Calvary.

During the period between the Testaments the Suffering Servant role of Christ was overshadowed by the messianic prophecies of judgment (cf. Mal. 4), so that even John the Baptist pointed to this latter ministry in his preaching (Matt. 3:7–12). And because Jesus adopted the role of the Suffering Servant, John inquired, "Art thou he that should come [*ho erchomenos*, the coming One, Messiah], or do we look for another [another of a different kind of Messiah]?" (Matt. 11:3). Note Jesus' reply (Matt. 11:4–5). It is in this light that we may understand Peter's reply to Jesus (Matt. 16:21–23). So obsessed were the disciples with the messianic role of judgment that they could not see the Christ as being crucified. Not until after the resurrection, and at Jesus' own teaching, did they comprehend his role as the Suffering Servant (Luke 24:44–46).

Jesus did not neglect to teach his mission of judgment (John 12:31, judgment here meaning crisis). Every time a man or a nation is confronted with Jesus Christ, it is a judgment or crisis. Judgment has been committed to the Son (cf. John 5:22,27; 9:39). In his first coming Jesus was the Suffering Servant. In his second coming he will judge all men and nations (Matt. 25:31 ff.; Rom. 14:10; 2 Cor. 5:10; Rev. 12:5; 20:11 ff.). Now he is the Suffering Servant, our Saviour; then he will be our Judge to reward the redeemed and to consign the unredeemed to everlasting suffering.

Vicarious Death

This simply means that the death of Jesus was not for himself but for others. It is the idea of substitution. Thus, Jesus did not die for any wrong that he had done or as a martyr to a cause. His death accomplished for man what he could not do for himself.

As a sinner man is under the condemnation of God's law. Within himself he is incapable of satisfying the demands of that law. So by God's grace his Son satisfied the demands for him.

This thought is present in the Old Testament. The sacrifice on the Day of Atonement clearly set forth the substitution of animals for the expiation of sin (cf. Lev. 16:1–34; note the scapegoat). Isaiah 53 pictures a man, not an animal, as the substitute ("for our transgressions . . . for our iniquities").

In the New Testament two Greek prepositions clearly teach the idea of substitution. *Anti* means one set over against another or in place of another. "The Son of man came . . . to give his life a ransom for [*anti*] many" (Matt. 20:28; cf. Mark 10:45). *Huper* means over, on behalf of, for, or as a substitute for. It sometimes carries the idea of one standing over another to take the blows meant for him. "For he hath made him to be sin for [*huper*] us, . . . that we might be made the righteousness of God in him" (2 Cor. 5:21; cf. John 11:50). Jesus used this word when he described himself as the Good Shepherd who gives his life *for* the sheep (John 10:11–15). Paul used it when he said, "Christ hath redeemed us from the curse of the law, being made a curse *for* us" (Gal. 3:13).

Substitution is seen in John 1:29. "Behold the Lamb of God, which taketh away the sin of the world." "Taketh away" renders the verb *airō*, to take up that of another and bear it as one's own (cf. Matt. 27:32). Thus Jesus took our sin and bore it on the cross as though it were his own.

The vicarious death of Jesus does not leave us without obligation. For we must in faith receive that which Christ has done in our stead. Else his substitution cannot avail for us.

Bodily Resurrection

With respect to Jesus this means that he rose bodily from the grave. With regard to others it speaks of a bodily resurrection at the end of the age.

Many attempts have been made to deny the bodily resurrection of Jesus. It has been explained as a grave robbery (Matt. 28:11–15), a legal removal by Joseph of Arimathea, a mistaken tomb on the part of the women, a fraudulent story on the part of the disciples, and a case of hysteria or hypnosis. It has been suggested that Jesus did not die on the cross but merely fainted and later revived. Even David F. Strauss, one of the most fanatical opponents of the resurrection of Jesus, denied this. Suffice it to say that none of these positions is held today.

The position most commonly held by liberal scholars today is that Jesus did not rise bodily. His resurrection simply means that his spirit survived death. If so, how may Jesus be regarded as any more than Buddha, Mohammed, or Gandhi? Such a view of the resurrection denies the very term itself. "Resurrection" means that something which was dead came to life again. No one claims that Jesus' spirit died, only his body. The spiritual resurrection theory is Platonic Greek philosophy, not New Testament Christology.

This does not explain the empty tomb. All four Gospels record that Jesus' dead body was placed in the tomb. Three days later the tomb was empty. All but Luke were eyewitnesses of the fact. Luke, a physician and reliable historian, after investigation (Luke 1:1–4; v. 3, "having had perfect understanding," literally, "having traced accurately") recorded the most beautiful and complete account of the bodily resurrection of Jesus. In all, the New Testament records ten postresurrection appearances of Jesus. How else can one explain the transformation wrought in the disciples?

In 1 Corinthians 15 Paul answers the Platonic philosophers who insisted on a spiritual resurrection. He thoroughly argues for a bodily resurrection. Four times he says that Jesus was "seen" (vv. 5–8). This word (Greek, *horaō*) means to see with the natural eye and to interpret and retain what is seen. Jesus was "seen" by Peter (Luke 24:34), the twelve (Luke 24:36 ff.; John 20:19), above five hundred (Matt. 28:16 ff.), James, and "all the apostles" (John 20:26 ff.). Finally, he was seen of Saul of Tarsus, the persecutor (Acts 9), who became Paul the apostle. Someone described Paul's experience as an epileptic seizure. We could certainly wish that we had an epidemic of such!

The resurrection body of Jesus was recognized by his disciples. He ate and spoke. Yet his body was not subject to time, space, thickness, or gravity (Luke 24:31 ff.; John 20:19 ff.).

The bodily resurrection of Jesus authenticates his deity (Matt. 12:40; Rom. 1:4), justifies the believer (Rom. 4:25), authenticates the gospel (1 Cor. 15:12–20), and is the firstfruits of that which ours shall be the general harvest (1 Cor. 15:23).

Ascension

Forty days after his resurrection Jesus ascended into heaven (Acts 1:9). Paul pictures his arrival in heaven as that of a returning conqueror (Eph. 4:8). The author of Hebrews says that as the crucified Saviour he entered "into heaven itself, now to appear in the presence of God for us" (9:24). His sacrifice is ever before God as an intercession for us (Heb. 7:25). This writer also records that he is seated "on the right hand of God; from henceforth expecting till his enemies be made his footstool" (10:12–13). Paul adds that he reigns in his mediatorial kingdom, subduing the universe unto himself (1 Cor. 15:25).

In heaven our Lord is the same Jesus his disciples knew on earth. He is still the crucified Lord (Rev. 5:6,12). He is one with his people on earth (Acts 7:56; 9:4). He is our mediator between God and man (1 Tim. 2:5; 1 John 2:1). He is our High Priest who can be touched with our infirmities (Heb. 4:15). He helps us in our trials and renders effective our reconciliation to God (2:17–18). He is "the same yesterday, and to day, and for ever" (13:8).

Jesus has not left us as an orphan in the world (John 14:18, literal translation). While on earth he said, "I will pray the Father, and he shall give you another [of like kind] Comforter, that he may abide with you for ever; even the Spirit" (John 14:16–17). B. H. Carroll called the Holy Spirit the "other Jesus." Marcus Dods calls him "Jesus' *alter ego*." He is with us to comfort, strengthen, guide, and empower us. As Jesus is our advocate before God (1 John 2:1), the Holy Spirit is God's advocate (one meaning of comforter) to us.

"So Christ was once [once for all] offered to bear the sins of many; and unto them that look for him shall he appear the second time without [apart from] sin unto salvation" (Heb. 9:28). "Even so, come, Lord Jesus" (Rev. 22:20).

Postascension Christ

Forty days after the resurrection Jesus ascended into heaven (Luke 24:51; Acts 1:9). Paul pictures his return to heaven as the triumphal entry of a conquering king (Eph. 4:8 ff.). Here he "sat down on the right hand of God; from henceforth expecting till his enemies be made his footstool" (Heb. 10:12–13). "Sat down" suggests our Lord's finished redemptive work, which contrasts with the unfinished sacrifices of the Levitical priesthood who "standeth daily ministering" (v. 11).

The New Testament does not list in order the events which transpired upon Jesus' ascension. But certain events are stated. He presented the blood of the sacrifice before the Father (Heb. 9:12,24). He prayed the Father to send the Holy Spirit upon his people (John 14:16). Through the Holy Spirit he endowed with spiritual gifts those who should serve him (Eph. 4:8 ff.; cf. 1 Cor. 12:1 ff.). In heaven "he ever liveth to make intercession" for his own (Heb. 7:25). Thus "we have an advocate with the Father [*pros ton patera*, face-to-face with the Father], Jesus Christ the righteous" (1 John 2:1). The word "advocate" means one who pleads the cause of another, especially for the defense. This does not mean that God prays to God. Rather it suggests that his sacrifice for our sins is ever before the Father as evidence of the atonement (cf. 1 John 2:2).

In heaven Jesus is concerned for his people on earth. When he entered heaven he "sat down." The first time thereafter when one saw him he was "standing on the right hand of God" (Acts 7:55). This suggests his concern for Stephen. He is identified with us in our suffering for him (Acts 9:4–5). When he returned to heaven he carried his human-divine nature with him. He is still "the Son of man" (Acts 7:56; Rev. 1:13). In his glorified body he still bears the evidence of his sacrifice

(Rev. 1:18; 5:6,12). He is still our High Priest who knows our infirmities. Thus we can come to him for help in time of need (Heb. 4:15–16).

At his ascension Jesus received again the glory which he had with the Father before the world was (John 17:5). Indeed, Paul says more. In Philippians 2:5–9 he speaks of Christ emptying himself. In so doing he did not lose any part of his deity. He poured it from one form into another—the incarnation. But in Christ's ascension, Paul says, "God also hath highly exalted him" (v. 9). "Highly exalted" means "exalted beyond." Beyond what? "Because of Christ's voluntary humiliation God lifted him above or beyond (*huper*) the state of glory which he enjoyed before the Incarnation. What glory did Christ have after the Ascension that he did not have before in heaven? . . . Clearly his humanity. He returned to heaven the Son of Man as well as the Son of God" (Robertson). Thus the name above every name—*Jesus* Christ. "Jesus," Jehovah is salvation. Thus now he is not only Creator but Saviour (cf. Rev. 5:9–14).

"Unto them that look for him shall he appear the second time without [apart from] sin unto salvation [glorification of the redeemed]" (Heb. 9:28).

Mediator

The word "mediator" (*mesitēs*) appears six times in the New Testament (Gal. 3:19–20; 1 Tim. 2:5; Heb. 8:6; 9:15; 12:24). It appears in the Old Testament (Septuagint) one time as "daysman" or "umpire" (Job 9:33). In Hebrews 6:17 the verb form is rendered "confirmed" or "interposed" (*mesiteuō*). The root word for these two forms is *mesos*. All three are found frequently in the papyri.

Mesos means "middle." *Mesitēs* may be rendered "the one in the middle" or the "mediator." This latter word is used of Moses as the "mediator" of the law (Gal. 3:19–20). In Hebrews it speaks of Christ as the "mediator" of the new covenant (8:6; 9:15; 12:24).

In classical Greek *mesitēs* referred to an "arbiter" or one who settled a difference between two people, thereby effecting a reconciliation. The office was also common in Roman life. It was sometimes used of one who went bail for another, guaranteed his debt, or was his surety for money borrowed from a bank. In matters of reconciliation the "mediator" must perfectly represent both parties. He must do all within his power to effect a reconciliation.

It is in this light that we can best understand 1 Timothy 2:5. Literally it reads, "For one God, also one mediator [*mesitēs*] of God and of men, a man Christ Jesus." Sin separated man from God. Hence the need for a mediator to effect a reconciliation. The English versions (KJV, ASV, RSV) read "one mediator between God and men." This suggests three persons: God, man, Jesus. But the Greek reads, "one mediator *of God* and *of men*" (author's italics). Jesus is the mediator who partakes of the nature of both God and man. Thus in Christ Jesus, who is truly God and truly man, both God and man meet in reconciliation (cf. 2 Cor. 5:19–21).

Jesus is "God with us" (Matt. 1:23) offering reconciliation. He completely identified himself with man apart from sin (Heb. 4:15–16). In his sinless life he fulfilled the demands of God's holiness. Knowing no sin, yet he became sin for us (2 Cor. 5:21). In his vicarious death he "gave himself a ransom for all" (1 Tim. 2:6). Thus in Christ Jesus, the "one mediator of God and of men," is effected a reconciliation. God offers it by grace; man receives it through faith in him who partakes of the nature of both God and man.

Lordship of Christ

The "lordship of Christ" means that Jesus Christ is Lord in every area of life—natural, physical, and spiritual. In the Greek version of the Old Testament, "Lord" translates "Jehovah" (6,823 times) and *Adonai* (340 times). The former is the saving name of God, the distinct name for the true God apart from all others; the latter denotes God in personal relationships. In the New Testament, "Lord" (*kurios*) appears 749 times. It sometimes means "owner" (Luke 19:16,23), "master" (Eph. 6:5), or "sir" (John 12:21). When used of Jesus by other than his followers it is a title of respect (cf. Acts 9:5). When employed by his disciples (cf. Acts 9:6; John 20:28), it is the equivalent of the Hebrew "Jehovah." (In between these references in Acts 9:5–6 Saul became a Christian.)

The words "Jesus is Lord" (author's translation) are a part of Paul's statement of the condition of salvation (Rom. 10:9). Here it is related to the fact of Jesus' resurrection (cf. Acts 2:23–24,36). Roman emperor worshipers said, "Caesar is Lord." To refuse to do so might entail death. Paul says that one must be so convinced that Jesus rose from the dead that he will risk death to declare him as his Lord.

One may well ask, "Can Jesus be one's Saviour unless he is also Lord?" Note that "Lord" precedes "Saviour" (cf. Acts 2:36; Rom. 10:9,12–13; Titus 1:4; 2 Pet. 3:2). Jesus warned that the lordship of Christ is more than mere words. It is a way of life for the Christian (Matt. 7:21 ff.; Luke 6:46).

The emphasis on the lordship of Christ among the first-century Christians is seen in the use in Acts of the divine term "Lord" (108 times) as over against the names "Jesus" (67 times) and "Christ" (31 times). Paul uses Lord 279 times; Jesus, 220 times; and Christ, 406 times. The emphasis was upon a living, eternal Presence. So the lordship of Christ is a recognition that the eternal Christ was incarnated in Jesus, who through his death and resurrection is the living Lord (Phil. 2:5–11).

He is Lord of the individual (John 20:28), Lord of the church (1 Cor. 5:4), "Lord of all" (Acts 10:36). A recognition and practice of this truth would solve every problem both personal and corporate within the Christian family. The climax of history will see Christ as King of kings and Lord of lords (1 Tim. 6:15; Rev. 11:15).

3
God the Holy Spirit

The Holy Spirit is the Third Person of the Trinity. As God the Father (First Person) revealed himself in human form (Jesus, Second Person), so he revealed himself in spiritual form as the Holy Spirit (Third Person). There is but one God, but he bears three relationships to nature and man. The Holy Spirit is a Person, possessing all of the attributes of personality. He should be referred to as "he," not "it."

The Holy Spirit is present in both the Old Testament (cf. Gen. 1:2; Psalm 51:11; 104:28–30) and the New Testament (cf. Matt. 1:18; 4:1; Acts 2:1 ff.; Rev. 22:17). But his work is more prominently set forth in the New Testament. B. H. Carroll called the Holy Spirit the "other Jesus." Marcus Dods calls him "Jesus' *alter ego.*"

The work of the Holy Spirit may generally be classified under revelation, incarnation, administration, evangelization, and sanctification. In revelation he inspired those who received the revelation (2 Tim. 3:16; 2 Peter 1:21). He illumines and directs those who seek to understand the revelation (John 14:26; 16:13). In the incarnation he was the divine power in conception (Matt. 1:18). He was present at Jesus' baptism (Matt. 3:16) and temptation (Matt. 4:1; Mark

1:12). Jesus' ministry was in the power of the Spirit (Luke 4:14-21). He went to the cross in the "eternal Spirit" (Heb. 9:14). He was raised from the dead according to the Spirit of holiness (Rom. 1:4). According to his promise the Holy Spirit came upon his disciples after his ascension (John 14:16-18; Acts 2:1 ff.). As Administrator, the Holy Spirit directed the spread of the gospel (cf. Acts) then, as he does today.

In evangelism he convicts lost people with respect to sin, righteousness, and judgment (John 16:8-11). By his power repentant and believing souls are regenerated (John 3:5). In sanctification he indwells the Christian as he grows in the likeness of Christ and in his service. The moment a person is regenerated, the Holy Spirit takes up abode in his life.

The New Testament knows nothing about a "second blessing." It is not how much of the Holy Spirit you have but how much of you the Holy Spirit has.

Speaking in Tongues

The New Testament phenomenon of speaking in "tongues" is recorded only in Acts and 1 Corinthians. The term applied to this phenomenon is "glossolalia." It appears to have been a temporary gift of the Holy Spirit (1 Cor. 13:8) designed to hasten the early spread of the gospel. Certain modern groups see "tongues" as an evidence of the baptism of the Holy Spirit. But what say the Scriptures?

The word "tongue" variously refers to the physical organ (Hebrew, *lashon*, Judges 7:5; Greek, *glōssa*, Mark 7:33) or to a language (Gen. 10:5; John 5:2; Rev. 5:9). It translates a Greek word meaning dialect (*dialektos*, Acts 1:19; 2:8; 21:40; 22:2; 26:14).

That speaking in "tongues" was an evidence of the power of the Holy Spirit is clear (Acts 10:46; 19:6). But these passages do not explain this meaning.

The first chronological reference to "tongues" in the New

Testament is in Acts 2. People of different languages were present at Pentecost (vv. 5,9–11). Filled with the Holy Spirit, the disciples "began to speak with other [*hetera,* other of a different kind] tongues [*glōssa*]" (v. 4). Each man heard in his own dialect (*dialektos,* vv. 6–8). It would seem, therefore, that the disciples without previous study were enabled to speak in languages other than their own, that the gospel might be heard by all those present on this particular occasion.

The second reference to "tongues" is in 1 Corinthians 12–14. Paul lists "tongues" among the spiritual gifts received severally by some members of that church (12:10). But others received the ability to interpret these "tongues" (v. 10). "Tongues" were not to be used as a display (14:6 ff.). To prophesy or preach clearly is better than speaking in "tongues" (14:1 ff.). Paul forbids to speak in "tongues" without an interpreter, so that all may understand (v. 5). He prefers to speak so that men may understand rather than by "tongues" (v. 19).

The ability to speak in "tongues" or "languages" other than their own was proof to the heathen that God was in their preaching (vv. 21 ff.). If they spoke in other languages not understood by their hearers without an interpreter, they appeared to them to be mad (vv. 23 ff.). Hence the need for interpreters.

Therefore, it appears that "tongues" was the ability for one to speak languages other than his own to enable the gospel to be preached quickly to all people. It was a temporary gift, not one of the greatest (14:5), which would fulfil its function and pass away (1 Cor. 13:8). The same ability today is derived through language study.

The New Testament knows nothing about the "unknown tongue." The word "unknown" (1 Cor. 14:2,4,13–14,19,27) is not in the original manuscripts. Note in the King James Version that it is in italics.

Interpretation of Tongues

One's position with respect to "tongues" will color his understanding of the interpretation of tongues. The writer holds that "tongues" was a gift of the Holy Spirit whereby one was able to speak a language other than his own, without previous study of that language. Therefore, "interpretation" would be simply the ability to interpret that language to those who did not understand it.

"Interpretation" renders a Greek word *hermēneia* which appears twice in the New Testament (1 Cor. 12:10; 14:26). The verb form, *hermēneuō*, is used four times (John 1:38,42; 9:7; Heb. 7:2). In each instance it speaks of rendering a word out of one language into another. Thayer gives the verb meaning as "to explain in words, expound . . . to translate what has been spoken or written in a foreign tongue into the vernacular." The root of this family of words is *Hermēs*, a proper name for the Greek god of speech, writing, eloquence, and learning. In Acts 14:12 (KJV) it is rendered "Mercurius," the Roman name of this god. It appears in Romans 16:14 as the name of a Christian.

In addition, the intensive form of this verb, *diermēneuō* (the word prefixed by the preposition *dia*, through), appears six times (Luke 24:27, expound; Acts 9:36; 1 Cor. 12:30; 14:5,13,27). It carries the idea of a thorough interpretation or explanation. The noun form appears once (1 Cor. 14:28).

Now, when we apply these thoughts to our problem, what do we find? The gift of "tongues" or languages was given to certain ones in order that those of that language might hear the gospel. Since in any group there might be those who did not understand the language in question, an interpreter was needed (1 Cor. 12:10). As the gift of speaking in other languages was a gift of the Holy Spirit, so the ability to interpret that language into others was a similar gift (v. 30). With some this gift, as others, became a vain display rather than a practical function (14:26). Thus it was a source of trouble in the Corinthian fellowship.

So Paul gives careful instructions as to the use of these gifts. Without an interpreter "tongues" are meaningless in edifying the church (v. 5). Therefore, when one speaks in "tongues" he should pray that one would interpret thoroughly what is said (v. 13). The literal meaning of this phrase, "that he [one] may interpret," is that speaking is with the design that one shall interpret (Thayer). If not, when one prays in a "tongue," those present who do not understand will not even know when to say "amen" (v. 16). When spoken in orderly fashion "tongues" would be an evidence to unbelievers present that God was in the phenomenon. But if no one interpreted to those who did not comprehend the language, those speaking would seem to them to be "mad" or insane (vv. 22–23). Hence the need for someone to interpret or expound thoroughly that which was spoken (v. 27). Without an interpreter they are forbidden to speak in "tongues" (v. 28).

The gifts of "tongues" and "interpretation" were temporary (1 Cor. 13:8–13). Today these abilities come through ardent study. Not everyone who can speak a foreign language can interpret it into another language. So in a sense "interpretation" is still a "gift."

Divine Healing

This New Testament phenomenon is receiving a revival of interest today. It is greatly emphasized in certain religious groups (cf. Pentecostals). Some of the older denominations (cf. Episcopalians) are studying it as a present-day possibility. Both the religious and secular press exhibit a growing interest in this subject.

There are four modern approaches to this phenomenon: metaphysical (disease is mental rather than physical, cf.

Christian Science); sacramental (by partaking of the sacraments, especially the Lord's Supper, healing power enters the patient, a modified psychological approach, cf. Church of England, Episcopal); psychological (some diseases are psychologically based; hence it holds that Jesus was no more than an unusual psychiatrist); historical-grammatical (recognizes divine healing in New Testament and holds that the church should practice it today).

Comments on the four: (1) The metaphysical ignores the reality of disease and suffering. (2) The sacramental has no scriptural basis. (3) The psychological, while containing certain basic principles, i.e., psychomatic medicine and values in psychiatric treatment, ignores the person and power of Jesus and the distinctive nature of his healing when compared with that of the secular psychiatrist. (4) Concerning the historical-grammatical, the New Testament teaches divine healing but not necessarily that the church today should practice it. What do the Scriptures say?

There are three basic Greek words rendered "heal." *Sōzō* sometimes means to heal (Mark 5:23; Luke 8:36; Acts 14:9) but generally refers to salvation. *Therapeuō* (cf. therapeutic) basically means to heal by natural means (Luke 8:43), but it is also used of miraculous healing (Mark 1:34). *Iaomai* refers to miraculous healing (Luke 6:19). In Luke 6:17–19 both of the last two words are used of Jesus' healing. In verses 17 and 19 *iaomai* is used, but in verse 18 *therapeuō* is found. Were these two kinds of healing by Jesus? Acts 28:8 speaks of Paul healing miraculously (*iaomai*). In verse 9 *therapeuō* is used. Ramsey sees the latter as done by Luke the physician. That is probably true here, but this distinction does not always apply. Both words are used of Jesus where miraculous healing is clearly the case.

The word used by Paul for the gift of healing (he never uses *therapeuō*) is *iama*, from *iaomai*, hence miraculous healing

(1 Cor. 12:9,28,30). It was a gift of the Holy Spirit, along with other gifts such as "tongues." Jesus healed out of compassion and as an evidence that the power of God was in his work (Luke 5:17). This power of healing he gave to his apostles for the same reasons (Matt. 10:8). Likewise, this gift seems to have been given to certain others during the first century. But like these other spiritual gifts (1 Cor. 12:8 ff.), it was to fulfil its function and pass away (1 Cor. 13:8). It was an evidence of God's presence in the Christian movement in its early or "child" stage (1 Cor. 13:11) to further the early advance of the gospel. After the apostolic age, Christianity was firmly established and needed no such ecstatic evidence. Medical and surgical healing still serves as an aide in missions, but it is through normal therapeutics.

All healing is divine healing as reverent doctors admit. It is not a question of whether or not God heals, but how he chooses to do so.

Prophecy

Prophecy is popularly associated with the foretelling of events. But the principal ministry of the Old Testament prophets (Hebrew, *nabi*) was telling forth for God. The first mention of a prophet in the Bible refers to Abraham (Gen. 20:7). The office may best be described in Exodus 7:1, the second time the word "prophet" appears. Aaron is to be Moses' prophet, or one speaking for him. So the prophet spoke for God. And while certain elements of prophecy dealt with the past and/or the future, the great body of the prophets' messages was telling forth God's will for the present.

The word "prophet" is derived from the Greek word *prophētēs*, meaning one who speaks forth. Not the time element but the function is primary in the word. Whether the prophet spoke of past, present, or future, he was telling forth for God.

In the New Testament the emphasis of the ministry of the prophet as foreteller gradually gave way to that of telling forth. John the Baptist was the last of a long line of prophets in the Old Testament sense of the word (Matt. 11:9,11). For he heralded him who was the fulfilment of the forthtelling of the prophets (Luke 24:27,44). Jesus was the "Prophet" in that he fully revealed or spoke forth for God, as well as foretold future events.

In the New Testament the element of foretelling remains (cf. Acts 11:27–28; 21:9 ff.). Certain portions of the Revelation are foretelling of events, but this book also spoke to its own generation and ours. Paul exercised the gift of foretelling (cf. 1 Cor. 15:51; 1 Thess. 4:14–18), as did Peter (2 Peter 3:10 ff.).

Among the spiritual gifts which Jesus distributed among his followers was prophecy (Eph. 4:11; cf. 1 Cor. 12:10). It would appear that this gift was related to telling forth the gospel in an especial way under the unusual power of the Holy Spirit. More likely, they were evangelists who went from place to place expounding the word. They probably differed from the apostles in that the latter seem to have been given more to opening new work. The prophets probably worked in the established churches and their environs.

Paul gives a greater importance to "prophecy" than "tongues" and other ecstatic gifts (1 Cor. 14:5 ff.). But even this gift was of a temporary nature (1 Cor. 13:8). It fulfilled its function and gave place to all who by the power of the Holy Spirit tell forth the gospel of God's grace in Jesus Christ.

Discerning of Spirits

The "discerning of spirits" is one of the spiritual gifts mentioned in 1 Corinthians 12:10. The word "discerning" renders *diakrisis* (a word from the verb *diakrinō*), meaning "to judge through" or "to judge thoroughly." It appears three times in the New Testament (Rom. 14:1; 1 Cor. 12:10; Heb. 5:14), but the verbal form is used nineteen times. In Romans 14:1 *diakrisis* is translated "disputations"—literally, "not to judge his doubtful thoughts." In Hebrews 5:14 it is rendered "to discern both good and evil." Thayer gives one meaning of the verb (*diakrinō*) as "to separate, make a distinction, discriminate."

So the idea of *diakrisis* is that of a judging between two things. This is seen in a breakdown of the word. *Dia* means "through" or "between," as of two things (cf. dialogue). *Krisis* is a "judgment," an opinion or decision given concerning anything, especially concerning justice and injustice, right and wrong. So a *diakrisis* is a judging, decision, or opinion between two things as to which is right or wrong. This use of the verb form is seen in 1 Corinthians 6:5, "one that shall be able to judge [*diakrinai*, infinitive] between his brethren" as to which is right and which is wrong.

When this is applied to the "discerning of spirits" the meaning is quite clear. Note that this gift is mentioned right after "prophecy" (1 Cor. 12:10). The Scriptures recognize the existence of both good and evil spirits. There is the Holy Spirit of God (cf. John 14:16-17,26; 16:13). Then there are the spirits of Satan (cf. 1 John 4:3; 1 Cor. 12:3 by implication). These under the power of evil spirits prophesied as did those under the power of the Holy Spirit. So to certain ones was given the power to discern or judge between these "spirits." That this was a needed gift is seen in such passages as Matthew 24:11-12; 1 Thessalonians 5:20-21; 2 Thessalonians 2: 2,9-10; 1 John 2:18-23; 4:1-6.

A. T. Robertson notes "a most needed gift to tell whether the gifts were really of the Holy Spirit and supernatural (cf. so-called 'gifts' today) or merely strange though natural or even diabolical (1 Tim. 4:1; 1 John 4:1 f.)." Christian people should discern the spirits today so as not to be taken in by charlatans or false prophets. This may be done through prayer and an intelligent testing of their claims by the Word of God.

We are told to "beware of false prophets, which come to you in sheep's clothing, but inwardly they are ravening wolves. Ye shall know them by their fruits" (Matt. 7:15–16; cf. Acts 20:29–32).

Miracles

The Bible assumes the reality of the miraculous. It records miracles in both the Old and New Testaments (cf. Exo. 7:9–10, ten plagues; 2 Kings 1:12; 4:34–35; Acts 3:1 ff.; 5:12; 9:32 ff.). The power to work miracles was a gift of the Holy Spirit (1 Cor. 12:10).

The Gospels record thirty-five distinct miracles performed by Jesus. He also wrought numerous miracles which are not recorded (cf. Matt. 4:23–25; Mark 6:56; Luke 6:17–19). Jesus never worked a miracle purely for his own benefit. Nor did he do so on demand (Matt. 12:38 ff.; Luke 23:8 ff.). The miracles of Jesus dealt with nature, healing, demons, and death. He himself was a miracle as seen in his virgin birth, sinless life, vicarious death, and bodily resurrection. The resurrection was the "sign" given to his critics as proof of his deity (Matt. 12:39 ff.), a miracle which they denied when it happened (Matt. 28:11–15).

The New Testament uses four words with reference to miracles (*dunamis*, act of power, mighty work, Matt. 11:20–23; *sēmeion*, sign, John 2:11; *teras*, wonder, Matt. 24:24; *ergon*, work, Matt. 11:2). The word "miracle" does not appear in Matthew (KJV). One time it is used in Mark (9:39) where it translates *dunamis*, and one time in Luke (23:8) where it renders *sēmeion*. In John it is found thirteen times for *sēmeion* ("sign" in Revised Version), signs of Jesus' deity. The Revised Standard Version omits the word "miracle" altogether, preferring to give literal translations to the various words. But the idea of the miraculous is everywhere evident in the Gospels and elsewhere.

Some deny miracles on the basis of natural law. True, God works by his laws in nature. However, the universe is not mechanical but personal. There are laws known to God which are unknown to man. Even at the human level the personal and spiritual are superior to the mechanical and natural. Who can deny to the infinite Spirit a knowledge of law unknown to finite beings? So what appears as unnatural to man is natural with God. Miracles are not merely magic. They are manifestations of God, who is both immanent and transcendent, as he employs powers known to God but not to man, as he achieves his personal and spiritual ends.

4
The Bible

The Bible is the divinely inspired Word of God. "All scripture is God-breathed," says Paul (2 Tim. 3:16, author's translation). It is, therefore, our one sufficient and authoritative rule of faith and practice. The Bible does not contain the word of God. It is the written Word of God.

Through men who were guided by the Holy Spirit, God has progressively revealed himself and his will to men. Progressive revelation does not refer to God's inability to reveal but to man's ability to receive. Thus, we find a greater picture of God in John than in Genesis. But the God of the one is the God of the other.

No one part of the Bible is more inspired than any other. But certain elements of God's revelation are more clearly seen in some places than in others. This is due not to God's limitation but to his divine purpose. For instance, God's redemptive love and will are clearly discernible throughout the Bible. But they are more clearly delineated in the New Testament than in the Old Testament.

Thus the New Testament is the fruit of which the Old Testament is the root. In this light Baptists accept both the Old and New Testaments as God's Word. But they regard the New

Testament as the final and fixed revelation of God. Through the Holy Spirit our understanding of it increases day by day. But its message is complete and unchangeable.

An old man asked a preacher to identify a leaflet which he had found. When told that it was a page out of the Bible, he said, "I knew that it was something special. For nothing I ever read affected me as it did."

Revelation

The word "revelation" means that which is uncovered. In Luke 2:26 "revealed" means to utter an oracle. The English word "revelation" (Greek, *apocalypse*) appears only in the New Testament (Rom. 2:5; 16:25; 1 Cor. 14:6,26; 2 Cor. 12:1,7; Gal. 1:12; 2:2; Eph. 1:17; 3:3; 1 Peter 1:13; Rev. 1:1). The verb "reveal" appears in both Testaments (O.T., *galah*, to be uncovered, cf. 1 Sam. 3:21; Dan. 10:1; N.T., *apokalupto*, to uncover or unveil, cf. Luke 2:35; Rom. 1:17–18; Eph. 3:5).

In the biblical religious sense "revelation" means the self-disclosure of God whereby he makes himself known to men. In one sense God reveals himself to all men through nature (Psalm 19:1; Rom. 1:19 ff.) and conscience (Rom. 2:14–15). The former is in respect to his power; the latter regards his moral and spiritual will. Man may receive or reject this revelation or that in the Bible. But he is responsible for the revelation which he has (Rom. 1:19 to 3:19).

The usual sense of revelation is that which comes through personal instruments (Isa. 22:14). It may be to and through patriarchs (Gen. 6:14 ff.; 12:1 ff.), prophets (Ex. 3:1 ff.; 2 Sam. 12:1 ff.; Isa. 1:1 ff.), judges (Judges 6:11), kings (Psalm 23), and apostles (1 Cor. 14:6; Gal. 2:2). Revelation is usually thought to be progressive. This does not refer to God's ability to reveal but to man's ability to receive. Thus there is a higher concept of God in John than in Genesis. But the God of the one is the God of the other.

The supreme and complete revelation of God is in Jesus Christ (Heb. 1:1 ff.). Jesus is the revelation of the eternal God in Christ in bodily form (John 1:1–14; 14:9; Col. 2:9).

God's revelation in Jesus Christ is primarily that of Redeemer (Matt. 1:21; but see John 1:3; Col. 1:16–17; Heb. 1:2). This is foreseen in the Old Testament (cf. Gen. 3:15; Psalm 22; Isa. 7:14; 53). But it is complete in the life of Jesus Christ. It is climaxed in his death and resurrection (Luke 24:46). It will reach its final goal in eternity (1 Cor. 15:24–28).

The revelation of the mystery of God's eternal redemptive purpose in Christ Jesus is clearly seen in Ephesians 3:1–11. This does not mean additional revelation beyond Christ. It is God's revelation to his apostle with respect to the understanding of the meaning of the revelation in Christ.

The record of God's full revelation is found in the Old and New Testaments. Beyond them there is no further revelation in the personal sense as is presented in the holy Scriptures. For a full understanding of revelation one must also consider inspiration and illumination.

Inspiration

The word "inspiration" comes from two Latin words—*in* and *spirare*, "to breathe." It means that which is breathed in. In the religious sense it is directly related to revelation. It refers to the divine "inbreathing" whereby God imparted his revealed truth through human messengers to be declared and inscribed to other men. Thus the holy Scriptures are the inspired Word of God.

The English word "inspiration" appears only twice in the King James Version (Job 32:8; 2 Tim. 3:16). In the former it properly means "breath of the Almighty." In the latter it means literally "God-breathed." Thus Paul says, "All scripture is God-breathed."

This inbreathing of divine truth is by the Holy Spirit. Peter says, "Holy men of God spake as they were moved by the Holy Ghost [Spirit]" (2 Peter 1:21). The passive verb as here rendered "moved" means to be carried or borne along as passengers on a ship (Acts 27:15,17). Thayer notes on 2 Peter 1:21, "of the mind, to be moved inwardly, prompted." Thus holy men, moved inwardly, were borne along by the Holy Spirit.

The inspiration of the Scriptures is shown elsewhere by such words as "Thus saith God the Lord" (Isa. 42:5; cf. 54:6,8; Hag. 2:4; Zech. 2:9; 7:13). Paul claims to speak by inspiration (1 Cor. 2:10 ff.; Gal. 1:11 ff.). The Revelation is a vision given by the Lord (1:1 ff.). Repeatedly the Bible claims divine inspiration.

Various theories are held as to the method of divine inspiration. The two principal ones are called the verbal and the dynamic. The former regards the human means as an instrument through which the Holy Spirit gave his exact words as found in the original manuscripts. The latter regards the method as the Holy Spirit inspiring the thought, leaving the human instrument free to choose his own words, with the Holy Spirit guarding him from error (cf. Luke 1:1–3). Both positions hold to the inerrancy of the Scriptures.

E. Y. Mullins points out a third position: "the experiential and practical method . . . much more concerned with the result than it is with the process of inspiration." Upon the result, there is general agreement among Baptists that the Bible is the inspired Word of God.

Illumination

The word "illumination" does not appear in the Bible. The English verb form is found one time (Heb. 10:32) rendering a word meaning "to give or to make light." In this sense it refers to regeneration. But the Greek verb (*phōtizō*) appears eleven times in the New Testament (Luke 11:36; John 1:9;

1 Cor. 4:5; Eph. 1:18; 3:9; 2 Tim. 1:10; Heb. 6:4; 10:32; Rev. 18:1; 21:23; 22:5) where it is variously rendered. But the idea present in each is that of divine illumination.

Illumination in the theological sense refers to spiritual insight which is imparted by the Holy Spirit. Sin darkens the understanding (Rom. 1:21). The Holy Spirit illumines it (1 Cor. 2:14–16).

It is impossible completely to separate revelation, inspiration, and illumination. E. Y. Mullins notes that revelation is usually accompanied by illumination, and inspiration is attended by both. However, in a stricter sense they may be distinguished. Revelation is God's unveiling of truth. Inspiration is receiving and transmitting truth. Illumination is understanding truth (cf. John 16:13). In the biblical sense revelation and inspiration were completed with the close of the New Testament. But illumination is a continuing activity of the Holy Spirit.

The Holy Spirit illumined the minds of the inspired writers of the New Testament (as in the O.T.), thus enabling them to recall and interpret the revelation which God had given in Jesus Christ (John 14:25–26; 16:12–13). He enlightened the early Christians with spiritual understanding (Eph. 1:18; Col. 1:9).

Revelation and inspiration in the scriptural sense are not bestowed on all believers. But illumination is bestowed on all Christians who will permit the Holy Spirit to do so. Thus the priesthood of believers becomes a vital and personal experience, as each one submits to the illumination of the Holy Spirit who guides into all truth as it was revealed of God through divinely inspired men.

5
Man

Both science and the Scriptures agree that man is the crown of creation. The Bible clearly teaches that man is a direct creation of God. Evolution remains but a theory, and the supposed "missing link" is still missing. (And in this writer's judgment it will remain so.)

God made man in his own "image" (Gen. 1:27). Since God is a Spirit, this has no reference to man's body. It is often said that man has a body and a soul or spirit. More accurately man is a soul and has a body. The body is mortal (Rom. 6:12), but the soul is immortal (Gen. 2:7). In the resurrection Paul speaks of the Christian receiving an immortal, spirit-governed, incorruptible body (1 Cor. 15:35–56).

Created in God's image man possesses a rational, moral, and emotional nature which corresponds finitely to these infinite qualities in God's nature. Man is endowed with free will, and thus he is responsible for his choices. He is not a pawn in the hands of fate. Nor is his conduct governed merely by physical forces apart from his will. Man is responsible to God for his acts (Gen. 3:9 ff.). Man is to have dominion over his physical environment (1:28).

In his original state man was created free from sin and

inclined toward righteousness (Gen. 3:2–3). But his free will made man capable of sin. It was in the exercise of this will that man fell from his sinless state (v. 6). Subsequently man was depraved in his nature and inclined toward sin (John 8:44). Depravity does not mean that all men are equally bad in their conduct, nor that there is not some good in the worst of men. It means that all men have sinned and have come short of the glory of God (Rom. 3:23). Thus man is lost from God (Luke 19:10). From the first Adam, man receives his depraved nature. Through Christ, the second Adam, man may become a child of God (John 1:12; 1 Cor. 15:22).

Someone said that the greatest thing about man is that he is seeking God. To the contrary, the greatest thing about man is that God is seeking him (1 John 4:10). Even the worst man is of infinite worth in God's sight (Matt. 16:26). God in Christ has opened the way whereby all men may become heirs of God and joint heirs with Jesus Christ (2 Cor. 5:19,21; Rom. 8:15–17). This they do by trusting in Jesus Christ, the Son of man.

Free Will of Man

The free will of man denotes man's freedom to act within the context of his own will and judgment. Otherwise, he would be nothing more than a puppet.

God made man in his own image (Gen. 1:27). Thus he is a personality with the power of choice (3:1–6). He is capable of a sense of guilt (v. 6) and is responsible for his choices (vv. 8–24; Jer. 31:29–30; Ezek. 18:2). God has revealed his will to man through nature (Rom. 1:19 ff.), conscience (2:14–15), and the holy Scriptures (vv. 17 ff.). His supreme revelation is in Jesus Christ (Heb. 1:1 ff.). But man is free to act according to or in defiance of this manifold revelation (John 1:11–12).

The doctrine of the free will of man appears to conflict with that of God's sovereignty. However, reason itself demands both, to say nothing of scriptural teaching. Both are facts of experience. The sovereignty of God must not cancel man's freedom, or else man loses his personality and is incapable of fellowship with God. God would become responsible for man's sin, a thought which is untenable with the very nature of God.

These two doctrines meet in the realm of law. God's sovereignty is expressed in his natural, moral, and spiritual laws. Man's free will must relate itself to these laws. A rebellious human will does not break God's laws. Man is broken on them. But living in accord with them man realizes supreme benefits and a blessed destiny (Rom. 1:19 to 3:31).

These truths are most clearly seen in the spiritual realm. God's sovereignty has decreed the penalty for sin and the provision for victory over sin. Man is free to receive or reject God's overtures of grace. But he is responsible for his response to them.

The goal of God's redemptive work in Christ Jesus is to bring man's free will into harmony with God's sovereign will. The steps of this process are justification, sanctification, and final glorification (8:29-30).

Sin

The basic words in the Bible for sin are *chata* (Hebrew) and *hamartanō* (Greek), both meaning "to miss the mark or target." The target is God's will and character. To miss it is to come short of the glory of God (Rom. 3:23). Other words for sin mean crookedness, violence, and fool. Sin is described as lawlessness (1 John 3:4), iniquity (Acts 1:18), wickedness (Rom. 1:29), and offense (4:25). At its root it is transgression (5:14) or disobedience (Eph. 2:2).

The tendency of man is to tone down sin. Psychology calls it maladjustment; biology, disease; ethics, moral lapse; and philosophy, a stumbling in the upward progress of man. But

God calls it sin. Man weighs or measures sins, but to God all crossing of his will is sin. The greatest sin is unbelief with respect to Jesus Christ (John 16:9).

There are several theories as to the origin of sin. One, based on the Greek concept of matter as evil, finds it in man's material body. Another relates it to man's ignorance or incompleteness. Two suggested plans of salvation—namely, self-denial and self-expression—evolve from these erroneous ideas. The most likely theory as to the origin of sin is that it is due to man's being a free intelligent being with the power of choice. This theory agrees with our knowledge of man, God, and the Bible. Sin, therefore, is in the will before it is in the act.

The biblical account of the origin of sin is found in Genesis 3:1-7. There man's free choice was confronted with God's will and Satan's will. The will of man obeyed Satan and disobeyed God. Hence the transgression. Thus sin separated man from God (Isa. 59:2). The Bible calls this separation spiritual death (Eph. 2:1).

The universality of sin is taught in Romans 1:18 to 3:23. Possessing a knowledge of God, man sinned against it as he transgressed the written law of God and/or the law of conscience in his heart. Thus man is lost and needs a Saviour. Infants and mentally incompetents are somehow embraced in God's grace. All others upon reaching the age of accountability are responsible for their sins.

The penalty for sin is death, both physical (Gen. 2:17; 3:3, 23-24; cf. Rom. 5:14) and spiritual (Rom. 6:23). Therefore, the "second death" is final separation from God in hell (Rev. 21:8).

As terrible as sin is, it offers opportunities to both God and man—to God in extending his grace to man, to man in accepting God's grace unto salvation (Rom. 3:23-26). Jesus Christ was manifested to destroy both the power and penalty of sin (1 John 3:8; cf. Rom. 8:1-2).

Unpardonable Sin

The unpardonable sin is set forth by Jesus (Matt. 12:22–32; Mark 3:22–30; Luke 12:10) and is inferred in 1 John 5:16.

The occasion of Jesus' teaching was his healing of a demoniac (Matt. 12:22). The people were amazed and believed (v. 23). The Pharisees scoffed, attributing Jesus' power to Beelzebul or Satan (v. 24). By a series of examples Jesus pointed out the unreasonableness of their position (vv. 25–30). Then he pronounced this awful sin (vv. 31–32).

What may be said of it? It was not a sin of impulse. It climaxed a series of reasoned rejections of Jesus. It was not a sin of ignorance but of knowledge. The people saw Jesus' miracle as evidence of God's power. The Pharisees saw it as a work of Satan. So fixed were they in their opposition to Jesus that they attributed an obvious work of the Holy Spirit to demonic powers. Thus Jesus said that they had blasphemed the Holy Spirit (v. 31).

By continued rejection of Christ the soul becomes so calloused as to be unresponsive to the convicting work of the Holy Spirit—thus no conviction, no repentance, no faith, no salvation. Some question whether this sin is possible now. The writer thinks that it is. Certainly persistent unbelief until death is unpardonable (John 3:18). Even in the midst of life a continued rejection may lead to an inability to respond to the convicting power of the Holy Spirit.

Those who feel that they are guilty of this sin are not. A sense of sin is evidence that one is still responding to the Holy Spirit. The one who has no sense of sin should beware. It is impossible for a Christian to commit this sin, for he has already passed from death to life (cf. John 3:18; 5:24; Rom. 8:1–2).

Jesus distinguished between blasphemy against the Son of man and blasphemy against the Holy Spirit (Matt. 12:32).

The one is pardonable; the other is unpardonable. Why? If one blasphemes or rejects God the Father, there still remains God the Son and Holy Spirit. Blaspheme or reject God the Son, there remains the Holy Spirit. Blaspheme the Holy Spirit, and there remains no hope.

Every lost person should beware, for God says, "My spirit shall not always strive with man" (Gen. 6:3).

Priesthood of Believers

The "priesthood of believers" means that every believer in Christ is a priest. According to the New Testament, Christianity has no priestly order comparable to that of Judaism. Instead, Jesus Christ is our High Priest (John 17; Rom. 8:34; Heb. 2:17; 3:1; 4:14–16; 5; 7; 1 John 2:1), and every believer is a priest (Rev. 1:6; 5:10; 20:6).

The priesthood of all believers involves both privilege and responsibility. The privilege is accepted, but too often the responsibility is rejected. Multitudes agree in principle to both but neglect that which each entails.

The privilege of priesthood means that every Christian may come face to face with God boldly with no mediator other than Christ (1 Tim. 2:5; Heb. 4:16). He can pray directly to God in Jesus' name (John 14:13–14). He can confess his sins directly to God (1 John 1:9). He can read and interpret the Scriptures as he is guided by the Holy Spirit (John 16:12–15). He needs no one else to make a sacrifice for him. His sins are forgiven through the one sacrifice on Calvary (Heb. 9:12). Christ, our High Priest, is ever in the heavenly holy of holies for us (9:24). In his death the veil separating the worshiper from God's presence "was rent in twain from the top to the bottom" (Matt. 27:51).

The responsibility of priesthood involves every believer's duty to witness to God's saving work in Christ (2 Cor. 5:17–20). A priest stands between God and man to bring them together in reconciliation. Israel was a priest nation to pagan nations (Ex. 19:1–8). In 1 Peter 2:5–10 Christian people are set in this same role. Note the similarity of language between these passages. In Matthew 21:43–45 Jesus took this function from the nation of Israel and placed it upon his followers. The priesthood of all believers is a great privilege. But do not forget the responsibility!

Prayer

The impulse to pray is almost universal among men. Even when marred by sin the impulse is still present. Satan may darken men's minds, but their hearts still reach up after God.

Man is made in the image of God (Gen. 1:27). Thus he is capable of fellowship with God. The highest expression of this fellowship is found in religion. And prayer is central in this relationship. The materialist denies the possibility of prayer on the basis of natural law. But when it is remembered that prayer is a fellowship between the infinite Spirit and finite spirits, prayer is not only possible but inevitable. Nor does natural law deny the possibility of answered prayer. Even at the human level illustrations abound of the superiority of the spiritual over the natural. God's greatest gifts are spiritual, not material (2 Cor. 12:8–9).

The Bible places great emphasis upon prayer. There are 169 references to prayer in the Old Testament and 165 in the New Testament. Compare this with 5 references to preaching in the Old Testament and 138 in the New Testament.

Prayer was central in the life of Jesus. Twenty references are made to Jesus as praying (Matt. 14:23; 26:36,39,42,44; Mark 1:35; 6:46; 14:32,35,39; Luke 3:21; 5:16; 6:12; 9:18, 28–29; 11:1; 22:40–44; John 17:9,15,20). The disciples, noting his prayer life, asked him to teach them to pray (Luke 11:1). He taught them the Model Prayer (11:2 ff.). Repeatedly he exhorted them to pray (Matt. 6:6; 26:41; Luke 18:1). They were to pray believing (Mark 11:24). They were to pray, not to or within themselves, but to God (Luke 18:10 ff.). They were to pray in Jesus' name (John 14:13–14; 15:16; 16:23–24, 26). This means to ask through his grace and in his will. There is no scriptural basis for prayer through any other means.

Prayer is to be of the heart, not merely empty repetitions (Matt. 6:5–8). It is not always just asking. It is communion, fellowship (Isa. 40:31), or even an attitude (1 Thess. 5:17). Sincere prayer at times may be but a groan in one's soul to which the Holy Spirit gives words (Rom. 8:26). The Bible speaks of hindrances to prevailing prayer (Psalm 66:18; James 4:2). No sincere prayer goes unanswered (1 John 5:14–15). God has three answers to sincere prayer: yes, no, and wait.

6
New Testament Church

The word "church" translates the Greek word *ek-klēsia*, meaning the "called out ones or assembly." In Greek life it referred to the duly constituted gathering of the citizens of a self-governing city acting within the framework of the laws governing democratic bodies (Acts 19:39). In the Septuagint, Greek translation of the Old Testament, it is used of the nation of Israel assembled before God (Deut. 31:30; cf. Acts 7:38; Heb. 2:12). Thus the word "church" involves respectively a local democratic assembly and a general theocratic assembly. Both of these ideas are involved in the New Testament concept of the church. In effect Jesus said, "The Greeks have their assembly, and the Hebrews have their assembly. I will build *my* assembly" (Matt. 16:18).

The word "church" is used 115 times in the New Testament. At least 92 times it refers to the local church (cf. Matt. 18:17; Acts 13:1; Rom. 16:1; 1 Cor. 1:2; Gal. 1:2). The idea of the church in the general sense is found in such passages as Matthew 16:18; 1 Corinthians 15:9; Ephesians 1:22.

The "church" in the generic sense includes the fellowship of the redeemed without respect to locality or time. In this sense the church will not become a reality until after the return of the Lord and the judgment (Heb. 12:23; Rev. 21–22), an assembly of all of the redeemed of all ages in a purely theocratic rule under God. The word "church" is never used in the New Testament in the sense of a denomination or of any segment of organized historic Christianity.

The greater emphasis in the New Testament is that of a local democratic assembly acting under the lordship of Jesus Christ (Acts 1:15 ff.; 2:41–42; 6:1 ff.; 11:1–18; 13:1 ff.; 14:27). The autonomy of the local church does not mean that a church may do as it pleases but as Christ wills. In the New Testament local churches co-operated in matters of common interest in the work of Christ (Acts 15; 1 Cor. 16:1–4). Local churches exercised discipline over their members (Matt. 18:17 ff.), excluding or receiving members, but always through the presence and under the guidance of Christ through the Holy Spirit (1 Cor. 5:4–5; 2 Cor. 2:4–11; 2 Thess. 3:6).

The ordained officers of a New Testament church are bishop, elder or pastor (same office, Acts 20:28), and deacons (Acts 6: Phil. 1:1; cf. 1 Tim. 3).

It was to the church that Christ gave his commission (Matt. 16:18–19; 28:19–20). The "church" is the body of Christ (Eph. 1:22–23) with Christ as its head (Col. 1:18). It is also called the "bride of Christ" (John 3:29; Rev. 21:2) and the "pillar and ground" of the truth (1 Tim. 3:15). Until Jesus comes again the local church is a "colony of heaven" (Phil. 3:20, Moffatt), a "sounding board" of the gospel (1 Thess. 1:8, Phillips), and a "fellowship" through which we are to carry out our stewardship of the gospel to all men. The person who despises the church despises Christ, for it is his body and bride.

Foundation of the Church

"Upon this rock I will build my church" (Matt. 16:18). These words were spoken by Jesus following Peter's confession, "Thou art the Christ, the Son of the living God" (v. 16). To what or to whom did Jesus refer by "this rock"?

The Roman Catholic Church regards it as Peter himself and upon this bases its claim as the one true church. Thus to them the church is built upon Peter and upon his successors, the popes. Peter did not so regard himself. He was one "elder" among others (1 Peter 5:1). The early Christians attributed no supremacy to him (Gal. 2:9–21). Non-Catholics deny this papal claim. Some Baptist expositors hold that "rock" refers to Peter but deny the Catholic position (i.e. Broadus and Maclaren). Maclaren says, "But it was not the 'flesh and blood' Peter, but Peter as the recipient and faithful utterer of the divine inspiration in his confession." But what do the Scriptures say?

Obviously Jesus' utterance is a play on words. "Peter" is *petros* (masculine), and "rock" is *petra* (feminine). *Petros* appears in the New Testament 162 times. It is a proper name save in John 1:42 where it is rendered "a stone." But the Greek text here makes it a proper name. *Petra* is used 16 times in the New Testament, always as "rock" (Matt. 7:24,25; 16:18; 27:51,60; Mark 15:46; Luke 6:48; 8:6,13; Rom. 9:33; 1 Cor. 10:4; 1 Pet. 2:8; Rev. 6:15,16).

Petros means a small stone broken off of a large rock. *Petra* means a ledge rock such as the foundation of a house (Matt. 7:24–25) or of a cliff (Matt. 27:51,60; Rev. 6:15–16). So the two words are not identical. Some insist that Jesus spoke Aramaic (a form of Hebrew) in which no such distinction appears. But G. Campbell Morgan points out that in the Hebrew Scriptures, "rock" always refers to deity, never to man.

So the play of words (*petros, petra*) suggests two thoughts. *Petra* could refer to Peter's confession (v. 16, Robertson). If so, Peter is a *petros*, a small stone broken off of the ledge rock (*petra*) and partaking of its nature. If so, it includes all who make such a confession of faith (cf. 1 Peter 2:5 ff.; "stone" here is *lithos,* a building stone). Or *petra* could refer to Jesus Christ himself. In the light of the Old Testament use of "rock," plus the New Testament use of *petra* with reference to Christ as the foundation stone (Rom. 9:33; 1 Cor. 10:4; 1 Peter 2:8), this appears to be the more logical meaning of *petra.*

So the church is built upon Jesus Christ (*petra*) out of those who confess him as "the Son of the living God" (*petros*), who thereby become "lively stones . . . built up a spiritual house" (1 Peter 2:5).

> The church's one foundation
> Is Jesus Christ her Lord (cf. 1 Cor. 3:11).

Nature of the Church

The word "church" is never used in the New Testament to refer to a building or a denomination. It is used only to refer to all of the redeemed of all ages and to a local body of baptized believers. The majority of its references are to the local church.

The church is a divine institution. It is built by Christ and upon Christ (Matt. 16:18; 1 Cor. 3:11). The New Testament speaks of "churches of God" (1 Thess. 2:14), the "church of God" (Acts 20:28; 1 Cor. 1:2; 1 Tim. 3:5), and the "churches of Christ" (Rom. 16:16). It was purchased by divine blood (Acts 20:28; 1 Cor. 6:19–20). The church "general" is composed of believers only (Acts 2:47). The church "local" is made up of baptized believers who are banded together to observe the ordinances, exercise spiritual discipline, and carry out the Great Commission (Acts 2:41–42; Matt. 28:18–20).

Many figures are used to express the nature of the church. It is "God's husbandry" (plowed field, 1 Cor. 3:9), God's family (Rom. 8:14–17), the "temple of God" wherein dwells the Holy Spirit (1 Cor. 3:16–17), the "pillar [stay] and ground [support] of the truth" (1 Tim. 3:15), a "colony of heaven" (Phil. 3:20, Moffatt), a sounding board of the gospel (1 Thess. 1:8, Phillips), and "candlesticks" or lampstands (Rev. 1:20).

The three major figures of the church are building, body, and bride. The church, then, is "God's building" (1 Cor. 3:9; cf. Matt. 16:18; Eph. 2:20–22; 1 Peter 2:5). This suggests God's indwelling of the church. It is the "temple of God" (1 Cor. 3:16). "Temple" is *naos* or the holy of holies wherein God dwells (cf. Jewish temple holy of holies, also Heb. 9:24).

The church is the "body" of Christ (Eph. 1:22–23; Rom. 12:4–5) with Christ as the head (Col. 1:18). It is an organism, not an organization. This denotes life and service. First Corinthians 12 pictures Christians as parts of the body of Christ, each with a specific function. The "body" is to grow into the likeness of the "Head" (Eph. 4:11–16).

The church is the bride of Christ (Rom. 7:4; 2 Cor. 11:2; cf. John 3:29). This symbolizes love and fruit-bearing. The church is to be subject to Christ as a wife is to her husband (Eph. 5:22–32). This figure pertains especially to the glorified church in heaven (Rev. 19:7–9; 21:2). All of these figures are highly suggestive of spiritual truth.

Men should be careful how they regard the church (1 Cor. 3:17, "defile" means "destroy"). For "Christ . . . loved the church, and gave himself for it" (Eph. 5:25 ff.).

Authority of the Church

Present-day church government falls into four patterns: autocratic, episcopal, presbyterian, and congregational. Autocratic means the absolute rule of one person. This is seen in the Roman Catholic Church (pope) and, to some degree, in the Greek (Catholic) Orthodox Church (patriarch). Episcopal refers to the rule of bishops (Greek, *episkopos*) as in the Episcopal and Methodist denominations. Presbyterian means the rule of the elders (Greek, *presbuteros*) as in the Presbyterian denomination. Congregational refers to the rule of the congregation as among Baptists and some others.

The New Testament pattern is that of the congregation. The congregation elected deacons (Acts 6:1–6), sent forth missionaries (Acts 13:1–3), administered discipline (Matt. 18:17), expelled members (1 Cor. 5:4–5), and received members (2 Cor. 2:5–8). While at times the local church worked through committees (Acts 15:6–21), the final authority resided in the congregation (Acts 15:22 ff.). The apostles advised and exhorted the churches, but each church determined its own course of conduct (1 Cor. 16:1–7; 2 Cor. 2:5–8; 2 Cor. 8).

New Testament churches were democratic bodies. "Democracy" comes from two Greek words meaning "rule of the people." Each person became a member by his own spiritual experience and decision (Acts 2:41; Rev. 3:20). Each enjoyed equal privileges and responsibilities (Matt. 20:25–27; Rom. 12:1–21; 1 Cor. 12). Each believer is a priest before God (Heb. 8:10–11; Rev. 1:5–6).

Baptists speak of the "autonomy" of the local church. "Autonomy" means "self-rule." Unfortunately this is sometimes interpreted to mean that a Baptist or a Baptist church can do as he/it pleases. Thus liberty becomes license (Gal. 5:13) or anarchy (1 Cor. 1:10). Self-rule is to be administered under the lordship of Christ (Matt. 6:10). Church and individual decisions are to be made under the guidance of the Holy Spirit (Acts 13:2; 16:6 ff.). Jesus promised his presence in church deliberations (Matt. 18:17–20). Paul said for the church to act "with the power of our Lord Jesus Christ" (1 Cor. 5:4). As members of the body of Christ each believer is to fulfil his function in co-operation with other believers (Rom. 12; 1 Cor. 12–13). So churches and/or individuals are not to do as they please but as Christ wills. We are to find the "mind of Christ" (Rom. 15:6; 1 Cor. 2:16; Phil. 2:5 ff.).

Freedom in Christ is not anarchy. Freedom involves self-discipline as well as self-expression. We are free, but we are free to co-operate under the lordship of Christ (1 Cor. 3:9). "Labourers together with God" means, literally, "fellow-labourers belonging to God."

Unity of the Church

"That they all may be one; as thou, Father, art in me, and I in thee, that they also may be one in us" (John 17:21). Here Jesus prayed for spiritual unity, not organic union. He and the Father were one in essence but two in outward manifestation. The oneness must be "in us." It must be the "unity of the Spirit in the bond of peace" (Eph. 4:3). Paul enlarges on this thought in Ephesians 4:11–16. The key verse is 13. "Till we all come in [into] the unity of the faith, and of the [full] knowledge of the Son of God, unto a perfect [mature, adult] man, unto the measure of the stature of the fulness of Christ." It is a unity of faith, based on a full "knowledge of the Son of God" and measured by the "stature of the fulness of Christ." This is not organic union achieved by a compromise of faith. It is inward spiritual unity grounded on a faith that speaks "the truth in love" (v. 15).

This is the pattern of New Testament churches. Each was a separate unity, ordering its affairs through democratic processes under the lordship of Christ. Without compromise they contended for basic truth (Jude 3; cf. Gal. 1:6–10; 2:11–21). But in Christian love they allowed for differences in presenting this truth (Phil. 1:15–18).

While each church maintained its individuality, the churches co-operated in matters of common interest without compromise of beliefs. The churches in Antioch and Jerusalem worked together in confronting a theological problem (Acts 15; Gal. 2). The churches of Greece, Macedonia, and Asia Minor co-operated in receiving an offering for the relief of fellow believers in Palestine (Rom. 15:25–26; 1 Cor. 16:1–4; 2 Cor. 8–9; cf. Acts 20:4; 1 Cor. 16:3–4). The churches of Asia Minor, and perhaps others, worked together in circulating the Scriptures (Col. 4:16). But in so doing each local church was free and responsible as to its own procedure.

Such is the pattern of Southern Baptists. Each church remains separate organically. Through voluntary co-operation the churches co-operate through associations, state conventions, the Southern Baptist Convention, and the Baptist World Alliance in rendering a Christian ministry and witness to the world. Each church is free to co-operate with other Christian groups in matters of mutual interest. But they do so, "speaking the truth in love," as they are led of the Holy Spirit to understand the truth (Eph. 4:15).

Apart from doctrinal differences, Southern Baptist church polity makes it impossible for Southern Baptists to enter into organic union with other bodies as presently constituted. These bodies accept into their "councils" only denominational groups. The Southern Baptist Convention cannot bind the churches in this or any other matter. So the churches continue to speak the truth in love, to co-operate where such does not involve a compromise of New Testament teachings, but to maintain the New Testament principle of free and independent churches.

Southern Baptists are an independent people who express their independence through voluntary co-operation.

Purpose of the Church

The purpose of the church is "the eternal purpose which he [God] purposed in Christ Jesus our Lord" (Eph. 3:11). It is God's age-abiding purpose of redemption made available to all men through Christ. Paul speaks of it as "the mystery of Christ" (Eph. 3:1–11). And it is to be made "known by [through] the church" (v. 10).

For this purpose Jesus Christ built his church. To it he gave "the keys of the kingdom of heaven" (Matt. 16:19). Note that "shall be bound in heaven . . . shall be loosed in heaven" reads literally "shall have been bound in heaven . . . shall have been loosed in heaven." Christ committed the "keys," the gospel, to his churches. Heaven has already decreed ("shall have been") that if the churches *bind* the gospel, failing to proclaim it, there is no other way whereby men can be saved (cf. Acts 4:12). If the churches *loose* the gospel, men who hear and believe it will be saved thereby.

Christ commissioned his churches to preach the gospel to, or to make disciples of, all nations (Matt. 28:18-20; Luke 24:46-49; John 20:21-23; Acts 1:8). He promised his presence and power through the Holy Spirit. And when the churches have followed him in world conquest, he has blessed their efforts.

The public ministry of Jesus was characterized by preaching (Mark 1:14-15), teaching (vv. 21-22), and healing (vv. 23-42). Individually and co-operatively his churches are to continue this threefold ministry in his name. But it is all to be centered in our Lord's redemptive purpose.

The purpose of the church is embodied in God's purpose of grace as seen in the doctrine of election. God elected a plan of salvation. He elected a people to proclaim this plan. This elected people is seen, first, in Israel (Ex. 19:1-8) and, second, in his churches (1 Peter 2:5-10).

The fate of Israel (Matt. 21:28-45) serves as a warning to the churches (Rev. 3:14-16). God's "eternal purpose" is at once our greatest privilege and our greatest responsibility.

Baptism

The New Testament church has two ordinances: baptism and the Lord's Supper. They are not sacramental but symbolic in nature.

The word "ordinance" does not appear in the New Testament with reference to either baptism or the Lord's Supper. "Ordinances" in 1 Corinthians 11:2 should be translated "traditions," or the teachings which Paul declared to the Corinthian Christians. "Ordinance" is used in connection with baptism and the Lord's Supper as acts commanded by Jesus. A Christian ordinance may be defined as a symbolic act commanded by Jesus to signify that which Christ did to effect salvation from sin.

"Baptism" comes from the Greek word *baptizō*, meaning "to dip, submerge, or immerse." It is used of Jesus being submerged in calamities (Matt. 20:22–23). But more often it denotes baptism in water. There are two different nouns in the New Testament which are translated "baptism." *Baptismos* refers to the act of baptism (Heb. 6:2; 9:10) with reference to Jewish ablutions or ceremonial cleansing. It appears only twice (not genuine in Mark 7:4,8). *Baptisma* connotes the meaning of the act and appears in the New Testament twenty-two times (13, John's baptism; 5, Jesus' suffering; 4, Christian baptism, Rom. 6:4; Eph. 4:5; Col. 2:12; 1 Peter 3:21). John's baptism was not synonymous with Christian baptism, since its meaning was different (Acts 19:3–5). John's baptism signified repentance and a readiness to participate in the kingdom of God. Christian baptism symbolizes the redemptive work of Christ.

Christian baptism, then, symbolizes the death, burial, and resurrection of Jesus. It also typifies the Christian's death to his old life, its burial, and his resurrection to walk in newness of life in Christ Jesus (Rom. 6:4–6; Col. 2:12). It also implies faith in the coming resurrection from the dead (1 Cor. 15:13 ff.). The New Testament knows nothing of infant baptism but that of believers only. Baptism in the New Testament is never by sprinkling or pouring.

Assuming that the subject of baptism is a believer, two

things are necessary for New Testament baptism—a proper mode and a proper meaning. The mode is immersion in water and emersion from water, a burial and a resurrection. The meaning is symbolic of death, burial, and resurrection. If the mode be changed, the meaning is lost. If the meaning be changed, the mode loses its significance. Hence, there is the widespread practice of Baptists in rejecting as New Testament baptism that which changes either the mode or the meaning.

In the New Testament baptism is the prerequisite of the Lord's Supper. It is an initiatory, symbolic ordinance and is to be administered "in the name of the Father and of the Son and of the Holy Spirit (Matt. 28:19, RSV).

Lord's Supper

There are four historic views relative to this ordinance. The Roman Catholic position is that of transubstantiation or "substance across." It holds that in the Mass the bread and the wine become the body and blood of Jesus. (Note: the New Testament does not say "wine" but "fruit of the vine.") Lutherans believe in consubstantiation. This view holds that the body and blood of Jesus are present with the elements of the Lord's Supper. Others hold to the view that grace is present with the elements, or that the partaker receives grace thereby which is not available otherwise. Baptists believe that the Lord's Supper is symbolic. The bread and fruit of the vine are but symbols of the broken body and spilled blood of Jesus.

The Lord did not state when or how often we are to observe the Lord's Supper. He instituted it on Thursday night, and the early Christians observed it on the Lord's Day. Any New Testament baptized believer is eligible to partake of the Supper. None is worthy except by the grace of God. The word "unworthy" in 1 Corinthians 11:29 is an adverb of manner, "unworthily." It refers not to the person's condition but to the manner in which the Supper is observed. The Corinthian Christians were making it a bacchanalian banquet.

The Lord's Supper is a repetitive ordinance. It is to be observed as a remembrance of that which the Lord did for our salvation (1 Cor. 11:24-26), until he comes again.

Baptists are sometimes called "close communionists." This is a misnomer. The "communion" is not between men but between God and man (1 Cor. 10:16). Here the communion is with Christ, not man. The New Testament name for this ordinance is the Lord's Supper.

Christian groups generally are agreed that baptism must precede the Lord's Supper. With this Baptists agree. The question is not "communion" but baptism. What is New Testament baptism? If anything, then, Baptists are "close baptismists."

Pastor

This is one of three titles referring to the same office. The other two are "bishop" and "elder." The qualifications for this office are set forth in 1 Timothy 3:1-7 and Titus 1:5-9. "Pastor" renders the Greek word *poimēn* (a shepherd). The verb form means to feed or tend a flock such as sheep (Luke 17:7; 1 Cor. 9:7). It is used with reference to the overseer or pastor (John 21:16; Acts 20:28; 1 Peter 5:2).

"Bishop" renders the Greek word *episkopos,* overseer. In Greek life it referred to one charged with the duty of seeing that things to be done by others are done correctly. In the New Testament it denotes one charged as the overseer of a local church (Acts 20:28; Phil. 1:1; 1 Tim. 3:2; Titus 1:7). It is used of Christ as the "overseer" of souls (1 Peter 2:25). "Bishop" never appears in the New Testament as one over a group of churches. It always is related to a local church office.

"Elder" renders the Greek word *presbuteros* which involves age (Acts 2:17). It came to refer to the dignity of age and wisdom. Among the Jews it came to denote members of the

Sanhedrin (Matt. 16:21; 26:47,57,59), who were usually older men. But its Christian use refers to one who presided over local assemblies or local churches (Acts 11:30; 14:23; Titus 1:5; 2 John 1).

That the three words refer to the same office is seen in Acts 20:28. Here Paul is speaking to the Ephesian "elders" (v. 17). In verse 28 he speaks of them as "overseers [bishops], to feed [as a shepherd] the church of God." So the three words—elder, bishop, and pastor—refer to the same office but to different functions within that office: elder (counsel, guidance); bishop (overseer or administrator); pastor (shepherd to feed, guard, and tend).

This relationship is clearly seen in 1 Peter 5:1–4: "The elders which are among you I exhort, who am also an elder. . . . Feed the flock of God [shepherd] . . . taking the oversight [bishop] . . . neither as being lords over God's heritage, but being ensamples to the flock. And when the chief Shepherd shall appear, ye shall receive a crown of glory that fadeth not away."

Deacons

Although the title is not used, the origin of the office of the deacon is probably found in Acts 6. The word "deacon" comes from the Greek word *diakonos*. It means literally "through dust." The origin of the word is questioned. One suggests the idea of raising dust in hastening to serve. The word probably comes from the verb *diakoneō*, meaning to be a servant or attendant, to serve or wait upon. This fits the service rendered in Acts 6. In any event "deacon" means a servant.

Jesus called himself a "deacon" or "minister" (Matt. 20:28). Likewise Paul referred to himself as the same (Col. 1:25). In 2 Corinthians 11:15 Paul refers to false apostles as Satan's deacons. The point in each case is that of one who serves another.

The original function of deacons was to "serve tables" (Acts 6:2). It was to relieve the apostles from this work that they might give themselves "continually to prayer, and to the ministry of the word" (Acts 6:4). That the office included more than a mere material ministry is seen in the fact that both Stephen, the first Christian martyr, and Philip were deacons (Acts 6:5). Both were also preachers of the gospel (Acts 6:9 to 8:5 ff.). There is no specific Scripture passage in which the present-day authoritative function is found, although Paul associates them with the office of bishop in his salutation in Philippians 1:1.

The qualifications for a deacon are found in Acts 6:3 and 1 Timothy 3:8–13. Note the similarity between the qualifications for bishop and deacon (1 Tim. 3:1–13). The bishops and deacons were closely allied in both qualifications and function. They are the only two ordained offices in a New Testament church. When both function properly, the work of the church prospers (Acts 6:7).

Missions

The English words "missions" and "missionary" do not appear in the Bible (KJV). They come from the Latin verb *mittere* meaning to send. The Greek equivalent is *apostellein,* to send forth. From it comes our word "apostle," the one sent forth. The idea of missions, however, is found throughout the Bible.

Christian missions is sharing the gospel with all men according to the command of Jesus Christ (Matt. 28:18–20). Paul speaks of missions as "the eternal purpose" of God "in Christ Jesus our Lord" (Eph. 3:11).

But missions is not confined to the New Testament. It finds its roots in the loving heart of God even before creation (cf. Rev. 13:8). Its first biblical note is sounded in Genesis 3:15, following the fall of man. The historical trail of missions begins with God's choice of Abraham (Gen. 12:1–3). Then came Israel, designed to be a priest-nation to bring other nations to God (Ex.19:1–8). But Israel forgot her divine mission. A major task of the prophets was to call the nation back to her mission (cf. Isa. 6). Finally, Israel rejected the Messiah. Thus Jesus said, "The kingdom of God shall be taken from you, and given to a nation bringing forth the fruits thereof" (Matt. 21:43). This "nation" of God's "in time past were not a people, but are now the people of God" (cf. 1 Peter 2:4–10). It is the people of Christ in all nations and all ages.

Jesus never thought of God's redeeming love as bestowed on one nation alone (cf. Matt. 8:8; Mark 7:26; Luke 19:10; John 3:16; 4; 10:39–42). He said, "And other sheep I have, which are not of this fold [Israel]" (John 10:16). "The field is the world," said Jesus (Matt. 13:38). Thus, following his resurrection, he sent forth his followers into all the world to disciple all nations (Matt. 28:18–20; cf. Luke 24:44–49; John 20:21; Acts 1:8). The book of Acts records the response of the first-century Christians to this command (cf. 13:1 ff.), and the remainder of the New Testament echoes the same (cf. Rom. 10:12–15).

History records that the grandest eras of Christendom have been the most missionary (cf. early Christian centuries). Likewise, the darkest era was the least missionary (cf. Middle Ages). The modern missionary movement began with William Carey, a Baptist (1792). The first American foreign missionaries were the Adoniram Judsons and Luther Rice, Congregationalists who on their way to India became Baptists.

In response to the missionary preaching of Luther Rice, the Baptists of the United States divided almost equally between the missionary and the anti-missionary groups. The former today is the largest evangelical group in the nation. The latter (Primitive or "Hardshell") is comparatively small in numbers. In 1964 the Baptists of the United States celebrate the one hundred and fiftieth anniversary of the founding of the General Missionary Convention of the Baptist Denomination in the United States for Foreign Missions (the Triennial Convention).

George W. Truett once said, "The church that is not missionary does not deserve the ground on which its building stands. For 'the earth is the Lord's, and the fulness thereof; the world, and they that dwell therein!'"

7
Salvation

The word "salvation" has many meanings in the Bible. In the New Testament it is used in the sense of rescuing from danger or destruction (Matt. 8:25; Acts 27:20) and of healing (Matt. 9:22). Its greatest use refers to making one a partaker of the spiritual salvation offered by Christ (Matt. 19:25; John 3:17).

Salvation in this sense has a threefold use in the New Testament: instantaneous, progressive, and ultimate. These three ideas correspond to regeneration, sanctification, and glorification respectively. The context in each case determines that to which the word refers. Failure to recognize this distinction leads to many errors, such as belief in salvation by works, falling from grace, and uncertainty as to one's "salvation" until one appears before the judgment seat of Christ.

Instantaneous salvation refers to redemption from sin (Acts 2:21; Rom. 10:10). This experience occurs immediately upon one's believing in Jesus Christ as one's Saviour. It is regeneration or the new birth (John 3:3–7). This is by grace through faith apart from works (Eph. 2:8–10). Thus believing, one becomes a child of God (John 1:12), a condition which is finished with no possibility of losing such a relationship. It is this condition to which we refer in the terms "security of the believer" and "perseverance of the saints."

Progressive salvation refers to the Christian's growth in grace, knowledge, and service of and for Christ (2 Peter 3:18; Phil. 2:12). This is related to sanctification or the salvation of the Christian's life (Eph. 2:10). Redemption is by grace through faith apart from works. Sanctification is a dedication to God's service by the Holy Spirit wherein, through good works, the believer grows into the likeness of Christ.

Ultimate salvation is the final culmination of the redemptive process or the total benefits and blessings in heaven (Rom. 13:11; Heb. 9:28). It is final glorification in heaven. It is for all of the redeemed, but the glory shall be in proportion to one's faithfulness in Christian service (Rom. 8:17). All Christians will be saved, but each will be rewarded in accord with his development in the Christian life. Each will enjoy heaven to the fulness of his ability (1 Cor. 2:7–9).

Atonement

The word "atonement" means just that—at-one-ment. The Hebrew word for atonement (*kaphar*) means "to cover." "Atonement" occurs only one time in the New Testament (Rom. 5:11) where it renders a Greek word (*katallagē*) meaning to reconcile. This same word in 2 Corinthians 5:18 is translated "reconciliation" (cf. Rom. 11:15).

So the basic idea in atonement is to make two as one, to reconcile a difference, or to bring together two persons who have been separated.

In his atoning work Christ has made reconciliation possible. God made man for his fellowship, a fellowship broken by man's sin. A holy God could not ignore man's sin. A merciful, loving God could not ignore man's plight in sin. In his incarnated being God was in Christ reconciling man to himself (2 Cor. 5:19–21). In his life, death, and resurrection Jesus satisfied the demands of God's holiness. He overcame the power of sin. He was both "just, and the justifier of him which believeth in Jesus" (Rom. 3:26). Through faith man receives this atonement as a gift of God's grace (Eph. 2:8).

Five theories of the atonement are worthy of note, none of which is fully satisfactory. The patristic theory, so-called as being held by many early Church Fathers, says that God paid a ransom to Satan for the souls of men. It has long since been discarded.

Anselm's theory (eleventh century and basic in Roman Catholic theology) says that sin violated God's honor and deserves infinite punishment. Since man could not pay the debt, Christ achieved excess merit for sinners. It is unsatisfactory in that it emphasizes God's honor and justice but overlooks God's love. It is external and mechanical rather than inner and vital.

Grotius' theory (seventeenth century) emphasizes God's government. Sin violated God's rule. To ignore it would endanger God's moral governmental principle. Through Christ's death God can forgive sin without peril to his righteous rule. This theory ignores God's infinite love which he would reproduce in man.

The Socinian theory (sixteenth century) is held by modern Unitarians. It says that Christ is simply a martyr to truth which should inspire others to moral struggle and victory; the only obstacle to God's pardon is man's lack of repentance. Also it ignores the power of the gospel to transform men.

The moral influence theory, held by many modern theologians, is similar in nature. According to it there is nothing in God's nature to be satisfied. Christ's death was to influence men to repent. It ignores God's justice and emphasizes his love.

Each of these theories falls short in that it emphasizes only a part of God's nature while ignoring the rest. To understand the atonement we must recognize that God is holy and right-eous; he is also love.

In the atonement God paid the ransom to himself. He satisfied the demands of his holy nature and moral law. Christ was both priest and sacrifice. He broke the power of sin and extended God's forgiveness to all who will believe in him. The fellowship is restored between God and man thereby. He promises final redemption to those who in faith look forward to his appearing (Heb. 9:28).

Conviction

This is the state of mind and heart whereby a lost person is brought to admit his sinful nature and practice. Apart from this experience there can be no salvation from sin (cf. Luke 18:9-14). Conviction is the work of the Holy Spirit.

The Holy Spirit reproves or convicts of "sin . . . righteous-ness, and of judgment" (John 16:8). "Of sin, because they believe not on me; of righteousness, because I go to my Father, and ye see me no more; of judgment, because the prince of this world is judged" (vv. 9-11). The Holy Spirit shows man the awfulness of sin and what it does, not merely to the sinner, but to God. He brings him to see that he is a sinner and that the greatest sin is unbelief in Jesus. He leads him to see that com-pared to Christ's righteousness his self-righteousness is as filthy rags (Isa. 64:6). Furthermore, he shows him the righteousness of God which is not by works but by faith in Jesus (Rom. 1:16-17; 10:3-4). Thus, man is led to admit the righteous judgment of God upon him because of his sin. He is thus ready to accept Christ or else reject him.

Conviction is not synonymous with salvation. Under con-viction man will either reject Christ and plunge deeper into sin (John 13:26-30), or else he will receive Christ as his Saviour (Luke 23:40-43). The man under deep conviction of sin is not far from the kingdom of God. But he should beware of a continued rejection of Christ, for God says, "My spirit shall not always strive with man" (Gen. 6:3). Without the Spirit there is no conviction; without conviction there is no hope of salvation. "To day if ye will hear his voice, harden not your hearts" (Heb. 3:7–8).

Repentance

The English word "repent" is of Latin derivation. Its basic idea is to "do penance." This is an unfortunate translation of the idea which expresses this vital experience leading to regeneration.

In the New Testament there are two Greek words translated "repent." *Metamelomai* expresses the emotional element in repentance. It means regret. It may be of a godly sort leading to genuine repentance (2 Cor. 7:8–10), a change of mind with no reference to sorrow (Matt. 21:29,32; Heb. 7:21), or merely regret that one got caught in his sinful deeds (Matt. 27:3). These are the only uses of this word in the New Testament. By itself the experience expressed in this word does not lead to regeneration.

Metanoia (the noun for repentance, used twenty-four times in N.T.), on the other hand, means a change of mind or attitude. It is more than intellectual since it involves the will or the heart (Mark 1:4,14–15; Luke 17:3; Acts 2:38; Rom. 2:4). While it may involve remorse or godly sorrow, its basic idea is a change in the direction of one's life (Acts 9:1–6). It involves a change of attitude toward God and sin: from hating God one comes to love him; from loving sin one comes to hate it. Repentance expresses a change of feeling, not simply with regard to what sin does to man, but also what it does to God.

Generally, *metamelomai* means sorrow after sin, while *metanoia* (verb, *metanoeō*) means sorrow before sin. In the latter one turns from sin to God, by his power to endeavor to walk no more in sin. Apart from this latter experience there can be no regeneration.

A contrast of these two words may best be seen in 2 Corinthians 7:10. "For godly sorrow worketh repentance [*metanoia*] to salvation not to be repented of [*metamelomai*]." Jesus said, "Except ye repent [*metanoeō*], ye shall all likewise perish" (Luke 13:3).

Confession

The word for confession occurs only 6 times in the New Testament where it is rendered "profession" (1 Tim. 6:12; Heb. 3:1; 4:14; 10:23), "confession" (1 Tim. 6:13), and "professed" (adjective, 2 Cor. 9:13). The verb form appears 23 times. It is variously rendered as "confess" (17 times, cf. Matt. 10:32), "profess" (3 times, cf. 1 Tim. 6:12), "promise" (Matt. 14:7), "give thanks" (Heb. 13:15), and "confession is made" (Rom. 10:10). The basic meaning of the word is to say the same thing, to give assent or agree.

Thayer points out the relation between profession and confession. "Profess" (Latin, *profiteor*) means to declare openly and voluntarily. "Confess" (Latin, *confiteor*) means to declare fully, as yielding or changing one's convictions. Thus with respect to Christ the word means to declare openly, to speak out freely and voluntarily one's change of allegiance from Satan to Christ (Luke 12:8). With respect to sin it connotates an open acknowledgement to God (1 John 1:9). Confession of sin with the idea of forgiveness is to be made to God, not man.

A classic use of the word is found in Romans 10:9–10. "If thou shalt confess with thy mouth the Lord Jesus [Jesus Lord], and shalt believe in thine heart that God hath raised him from the dead, thou shalt be saved. For with the heart man believeth unto righteousness [justification]; and with the mouth confession is made unto salvation." Here "confession" is more than saying some words. It involves the conviction that by his resurrection Jesus is Lord to such a degree that you will stake your life and soul on it. In Paul's day pagan worshipers said, "Caesar is lord." To refuse was to risk death. Many Christians paid with their lives to say instead, "Jesus is Lord." Confession, then, involves the complete loyalty of one's life to Christ. It is an open, voluntary espousal of Christ as one's Saviour and Lord.

Note that in Romans 10:9 Paul puts confession before faith. His emphasis is on open confession. In Romans 10:10 he reverses the order—faith, then confession—the proper sequence. We confess what we have already believed, as it becomes the outward expression of an inner experience.

The New Testament holds forth no case for "secret" discipleship (Matt. 10:32–33). One should not place his hope in such.

Faith

The vital place of faith in the Christian experience is seen in the fact that it appears (verb and noun) in the New Testament 492 times. It involves an intellectual assent to the facts of the atoning work of Christ. But it involves more—an act of the will.

The root verb for faith may be translated "to believe, to commit, or to trust." All three ideas are present in the word "faith"—believing what is written about Christ, trusting in him and his work for salvation, and committing one's self to him. One is to believe in or on Christ (John 3:16; Acts 16:31), not merely about him. John 3:14–18,36 is one of the greatest passages in the New Testament regarding this experience (cf. also John 5:24). Faith is one of the key words in the book of Hebrews.

In Romans 1:17 Paul says that man's justification is "from faith to faith" or a matter of faith from beginning to end. In chapter 4 Paul contrasts faith and works, showing that by faith alone can one be justified (v. 5; cf. also 5:1; Eph. 2:8–10).

Some would see a contradiction between Paul's writings (cf. Romans 4:3) and James 2:20–26. But there is no conflict. Paul sees faith as the cause; James's words regard the effect. Paul says that one is saved by grace through faith apart from works. James says that one shows his faith by his works. Neither teaches salvation itself by works. "The just [justified one] shall live by his faith" (Hab. 2:4) is the only verse from the Old Testament quoted three times in the New Testament (Rom. 1:17; Gal. 3:11; Heb. 10:38).

Unbelief means "no faith." In Heb. 3:12, for example, unbelief refers not to a loss of faith regarding one's redemption. The Israelites did not "unbelieve" as to their redemption from Egyptian bondage. They had "no faith" to believe that God could lead them into the land of Canaan. By comparison this does not refer to "unbelieving," to a loss of one's redemption. It means "no faith" to believe that God in Christ can lead the redeemed into Christian growth and service. Unbelief or "no faith" in Jesus as Saviour is regarded as the worst of sins (John 3:18).

Conversion or Regeneration

The effect of conviction, repentance, and faith is called "conversion." It refers to the outward evidence of an inward change. The word "conversion" occurs only one time in the Bible (Acts 15:3). But the verb form occurs thirty-nine times in the New Testament. It is translated variously as "turn" (Luke 1:16–17), "be converted" (Matt. 13:15), "return" (Luke 17:31), "turn about" (John 21:20), "turn again" (Mark 13:16), and "come again" (James 5:19–20).

In the spiritual sense conversion is the outward, direct result of the inward change of mind or attitude involved in repentance. The inner experience is repentance and faith. The outward evidence is a turning from the old life of rebellion against God to one of service to God (cf. Matt. 3:8; 7:16,20; Acts 9:1–22). Conversion is not the whole of the Christian experience. It is not the end but the beginning. E. Y. Mullins calls conversion "the Christian life in germ." In it is concentrated all of the elements of the Christian life which follows. We are not converted by our works, but our works are an evidence of our conversion (cf. Eph. 2:8–10; James 2:14 ff.).

The experience of conversion may vary with respect to age, personality, or degree of sin in one's preconversion life. A conversion may come as the result of religious training and guidance. It may be a crisis experience. But it will be definite. No two conversions will fit exactly the same mold. But three things are necessary for a genuine conversion experience: turning from self and sin; trust in God through Christ; the direct action of God's grace upon the soul through Christ and by the power of the Holy Spirit.

The word "convert" is also used in the New Testament in the sense of the reconsecration of the Christian (Luke 22:31–32).

Regeneration is the work wrought by the Holy Spirit in the unbeliever's heart as the result of conviction, repentance, faith, and conversion. The word "regeneration" occurs only twice in the New Testament. In Matthew 19:28 it has an eschatological sense, referring to the final redemption of the universe. In Titus 3:5 it refers to the redemption of the soul. In this context the phrase is "the washing of regeneration, and renewing of the Holy Ghost [Spirit]." Note that "washing" refers to inner cleansing, not baptism (cf. Eph. 5:26, cleansing "by the word" or word of God). The soul is cleansed of sin and made new or fresh by the Holy Spirit. Had Paul meant "baptism" he could have used the word.

In regeneration the penitent believer receives a new nature. This involves a moral and spiritual renewal of the will, aim, and purpose of life. Through regeneration God imparts to us his nature. Thus we are said to be "new creations" (2 Cor. 5:17, literal translation). Regeneration is an act of God, not of man (John 1:13). Since it is by grace, it obviously cannot be produced, aided, or completed by baptism. Baptism is the symbol of the experience, not its source or means (Rom. 6:4–5).

The idea of "new birth" is clearly set forth in John 3. The words used are "born again" or "born from above" (*anōthen,* anew, again, from above). They denote the spiritual change wrought by the Holy Spirit whereby a child of Satan becomes a child of God.

New birth clearly involves being "born from above." In the natural birth we are born in sin or with a sinful nature (Psalm 51:5; John 8:44). It is, therefore, necessary to be born from above if we are to become sons of God possessing his nature (John 1:12–13).

Furthermore, the "new birth" speaks of being "born again" or "anew." In the natural birth we were born into certain relationships: family and nation. After birth we achieve certain status: ability, learning, wealth, position in society. None of these entitles us to being citizens of the kingdom of God (cf. John 3:3). We must be born all over again or anew.

An analysis of John 3 suggests the issue to be a contrast between the natural and the spiritual birth (cf. vv. 3–7). Nicodemus thought of the natural birth; Jesus spoke of the spiritual birth. "Born of water" refers not to baptism but to the water birth or that which accompanies the natural birth. So Jesus says that before one can be born again (spiritual) he must be born the first time (natural).

The word "adoption" is a term used only by Paul in the New Testament (Rom. 8:15,23; 9:4; Gal. 4:5; Eph. 1:5). It renders a Greek word *huiothesia*—from *huios* (son) and *tithēmi* (I place)—thus a placing in the position of a son.

It is found on inscriptions and in the papyri in this sense.

In the New Testament "adoption" is used in three distinct ways: (1) the adoption of the nation Israel as chosen of God for his service (Rom. 9:4), (2) the adoption of believers as sons of God (Rom. 8:15; Gal. 4:5; Eph. 1:5), (3) the final redemption of the body in the resurrection (Rom. 8:23)—the complete redemption of both soul and body.

Adoption was a common practice among the Romans. To legalize the event certain people had to be present: the owner (in the case of a slave) or natural father, the purchaser, the weigher of money (uncoined metal), and no less than five witnesses. The adopted "son" severed all former relationships, and his "father" assumed his debts. In the eyes of the law the "son" became a new creature. He was "born again" into a new family. He received all the rights and privileges of a natural-born son, and he became with him a joint heir of his new father.

This custom is evident in Paul's use of the word "adoption" (cf. Rom. 8:15; Gal. 4:5; Eph. 1:5). The unbeliever is a slave to sin (cf. "spirit of bondage," Rom. 8:15; "under the law," Gal. 4:5). He is redeemed from the law (Gal. 4:5; cf. ceremony of purchase). Thus he receives, not earns, the "adoption of sons" (Gal. 4:5) whereby he cries, "Abba, Father" (Rom. 8:15). Note that the Holy Spirit witnesses or affirms the transaction (Rom. 8:15–16,23; Gal. 4:6; Eph. 1:5,13–14).

The figure of "adoption" should not be confused with a purely legal transaction. For Paul clearly sets forth the atonement wrought in Christ (Rom. 8:3–4; Gal. 4:4–5), the faith of the believer (Gal. 3:11–14; Eph. 1:12–13), and the work of the Holy Spirit (Rom. 8:14–27; Gal. 4:6; Eph. 1:13–14).

The words "conversion," "regeneration," "new birth," and "adoption" point to the same experience. The New Testament uses this variety of terms to refer to a change so vital that no single word can adequately describe it.

Righteousness

"Righteousness" when used of God refers to his holiness (Rom. 3:5,25); when used of Christ it denotes his moral perfection or sinlessness (John 16:8,10); when used of man it connotes that which God demands or that condition which is acceptable to God (Matt. 6:33). The Jews thought of this righteousness in terms of works of the law (Rom. 10:3), a righteousness which they could not achieve (Matt. 5:20).

Righteousness is one of the great words of the New Testament, appearing 92 times. It is akin to justification which appears only twice (Rom. 4:25; 5:18). But righteousness means the state of being "justified."

The theme of Romans is the God-kind-of-righteousness (1:17). The word "righteousness" appears in this book 36 times. Here righteousness is not an attribute of God. It is his activity whereby God declares man righteous or justified. This word belongs to a family of Greek nouns which do not describe what one is but what one is declared to be. So man within himself is not righteous. God declares him to be righteous as though he had not sinned. This he does because of the "righteousness of God" which is in Christ Jesus (10:3–10).

This righteousness is put down to man's account (4:3) because of his faith in Christ (John 1:12). Paul says that it is "from faith to faith" (Rom. 1:17) or a matter of faith from beginning to end. Man is not saved by works but by grace. As a Christian he is to walk in good works (Eph. 2:8–10). But he becomes righteous or justified through a judicial act of God made possible because of his grace in Christ and man's faith therein. Only thus may one become righteous before God.

Sanctification

The basic meaning of the word "sanctification" is dedication. It refers to that which is set apart for holy uses or for the service of God. It is akin to the word "holy." Originally, the word "holy" carried no moral concept. It acquired this as it became related to a righteous God. In pagan religions even immoral people used in the worship of their gods were called "holy." In the Christian sense "holiness" means "wholeness" or that which God intends for his people to be.

In the Old Testament the words "sanctify" and "holy" are used with reference to those things related to the service of Jehovah: temple, altar, vessels, people, and days. In the New Testament they refer primarily to people.

Sanctification is the realization of God's full will for one's life (1 Thess. 4:3–4; cf. 1 Cor. 1:30). It begins with a personal faith in Jesus Christ as Saviour. At that moment the Christian is sanctified in that he is dedicated to God and his service. All Christians are called "saints" or "sanctified ones" in the New Testament (Acts 9:13; Rom. 1:7; 1 Cor. 1:2; Phil. 1:1). This is a work of the Holy Spirit (John 3:5). Thereafter, through the Holy Spirit the Christian progressively grows in grace, knowledge, and service of and for Christ (2 Peter 3:18). Thus the instrument in this experience from beginning to end is the Holy Spirit (Rom. 8:1–17,26–27; 2 Thess. 2:13–14; 1 Peter 1:2).

The basic thought in sanctification is not that of ridding one's self of sin. Jesus, who had no sin, sanctified himself (John 17:19). He "dedicated" himself to God's will and work on the cross. However, as a sinful being, for the Christian sanctification does involve a progressive riddance from sin. The more dedicated he becomes the less place sin will have in his life (Rom. 6:11 ff.). But so long as he is in the flesh, the Christian will struggle between sin and righteousness (7:14–23). In Christ the Christian is freed from the power of sin (v. 24 to 8:2). But the New Testament holds forth no such thing as sinless perfection in this life (1 John 1:7–10). Such will be realized when we are completely sanctified or glorified in heaven.

This, however, is no excuse for carnal living. The Christian life is the sanctified life. And it becomes progressively so as the Christian yields himself to Christ and his service through the power of the Holy Spirit.

Perseverance

In a statement entitled "Baptist Faith and Message," adopted by the Southern Baptist Convention in 1963, are the following words under "God's Purpose of Grace": "All true believers endure to the end. Those whom God has accepted in Christ, and sanctified by his Spirit, will never fall away from the state of grace, but shall persevere to the end. Believers may fall into sin through neglect and temptation, whereby they grieve the Spirit, impair their graces and comforts, bring reproach on the cause of Christ, and temporal judgments on themselves, yet they shall be kept by the power of God through faith unto salvation."

This concept is sometimes called the "security of the believer" or "once saved, always saved." Scripture passages to this effect abound (John 10:28–29; Rom. 5:9–10; 8:30; 9:11,16). Read John 5:24. Note that the verbs "heareth," "believeth," and "hath" are present tenses. The only future thought is "shall not come into condemnation." Even this verb is a present tense with a future effect. The only past tense is "passed from death unto life"—referring to the moment one truly believes or trusts in Christ as Saviour. The words "everlasting life" mean "life of the ages" or "age-abiding life." They can mean nothing else.

Ephesians 2:8–10 is worthy of note. Literally, "For by grace have ye been saved through faith." "Grace" is a gift or unmerited favor. Note "not of yourselves: it is the gift of God: Not of works, lest any man should boast. For we are his workmanship, created [an act of God only] in Christ Jesus unto [not by] good works." "Have ye been saved" is a perfect passive tense meaning an action in the past, done to one by another, which continues and will continue in the future. It speaks of a finished work. Redemption in the beginning depends upon what God does, not man. Its permanence likewise depends upon what God has done and continues to do, not man. But note "good works, which God hath before ordained that we should walk in them." Good works are to be the fruit of salvation but not its root (cf. John 15:16). "By their fruits ye shall know them" (cf. Matt. 7:16,20).

In Jesus' high priestly prayer (John 17), he prayed, "Those that thou gavest me *I have kept*" (v. 12, author's italics). Though men may be faithless, he is faithful. To that end the Scriptures teach the ultimate salvation of all who believe in Jesus (Rom. 13:11; 1 Thess. 5:9; Heb. 9:28). There will be degrees of reward in heaven for the saved according to their works, but all true believers will be saved by God's grace (Luke 12:47–48; 1 Cor. 3:11–15). And all who truly trust in Jesus shall be with him in glory. The message of Revelation is the victory of Christ and the believer's victory in him. "Now is come salvation . . . for the accuser [Satan] of our brethren is cast down" (Rev. 12:10).

Perseverance does not mean that all church members will be saved but all true believers (1 John 2:19). Nor does it mean that true believers will never sin again. But sin will not be the habit of their lives (1 John 1:6–10). The Lord chastens his own (1 Cor. 11:32), but when we repent (Matt. 26:70–75; John 21:15 ff.) and confess our sins he always forgives (1 John 1:9).

"Falling from grace" (Gal. 5:4; cf. Heb. 12:15) does not mean to lose a salvation which you already have. It means "falling out of grace" or leaving the sphere of grace for the sphere of law. To seek salvation by works is to fall away from the way of salvation by grace.

Glorification

The term "glorification" refers to the ultimate and complete salvation which shall be realized in heaven. This does not mean that one is not saved in the sense of redemption until he gets to heaven. Redemption or regeneration occurs the second one trusts in Jesus as Saviour (John 1:12; 3:3). Sanctification is also an instantaneous act at the moment of regeneration, but it involves the process by which the redeemed one grows in grace, knowledge, and service of and for Christ (2 Peter 3:18, Eph. 4:13). Glorification is the culmination of this process in heaven (Heb. 9:28).

Paul speaks of Christians as being "heirs of God, and joint-heirs with Christ; if so be that we suffer with him, that we may be also glorified together. For I reckon that the sufferings of this present time are not worthy to be compared with the glory which shall be revealed in us" (Rom. 8:17–18).

Through his sanctification or dedication to the cross Jesus received the glory which was his before the world was (John 17:5,19; Phil. 2:5–11). While one's sufferings are not comparable to those of Jesus on the cross, the Christian is to suffer in finite degree in his service as did Jesus infinitely in his earthly life (Col. 1:24). This suffering is involved in the Christian's sanctification. He, then, is not only heir to Christ's glory but to his suffering as well (Rom. 8:17). And his degree of glory will be in proportion to his degree of dedication. The Bible teaches degrees of reward in heaven (Matt. 25:14–30; Luke 19:12–27).

All the redeemed will be saved in heaven. Some will be saved "as by fire" (1 Cor. 3:14–15); their useless works will be burned. Each will enjoy heaven to the full degree of his capacity. But the reward of one will be greater than that of another, according to his fruit bearing while on earth.

All Christians will share in the glory of Christ in heaven (Rev. 4:11; 5:5–14; 20–21). Mortal man cannot conceive of this glory. "But as it is written, Eye hath not seen, nor ear heard, neither have entered into the heart of man, the things which God hath prepared for them that love him" (1 Cor. 2:7–9; 2 Cor. 4:6–7).

Election or Predestination

The doctrine of election is one of the most vital in the Bible. It is also one of the most misunderstood. The word "election" does not appear in the Old Testament (KJV) and is found only in six verses of the New Testament (Rom. 9:11; 11:5,7,28; 1 Thess. 1:4; 2 Peter 1:10). The word "elect" appears four times in the Old Testament and sixteen times in the New Testament. The word translated "elect" is sometimes rendered "chosen."

The noun "predestination" does not appear in the Bible (KJV). The verb "predestinate" occurs four times (Rom. 8:29–30; Eph. 1:5,11). But the Greek verb which it translates is found six times. In Acts 4:28 it is rendered "determined before"; in 1 Corinthians 2:7 it reads "ordained." Where the verb "predestinate" is used in the King James Version, the American Standard Version employs "foreordain." The English word "predestinate" is derived from the Latin *praedestinare, prae* (before), and *destinare* (to destine). But the Greek verb is *proorizō,* to mark out or determine beforehand.

"Election" or "predestination" does not mean that God acts out of his own will to the neglect of man's will. Nor does it refer to the salvation of a few or the election of individuals. It is no excuse for fatalism. Election is not mechanical. It involves a God who is love and a man who is morally responsible. It never appears in the Bible as a violation of human will.

Thus there are two elements involved in election. God is sovereign in that he can do that which he wills and which is in accord with his nature. He is not only omnipotent; he is love. Furthermore, man, made in God's image, possesses free will.

He has the power of choice (Gen. 3:1–6), is capable of a sense of guilt (Gen. 3:7), and is responsible for his choices (Gen. 3:8–24). To our finite minds God's sovereignty and man's free will appear to conflict. But in the infinite mind of God there is no conflict.

E. Y. Mullins describes the God side of election. He "keeps the reins of government in his hands. He guides the universe to his own glorious end. That end embodies the highest ideals of holiness and love." But on the man side, man by his free will may accept or reject God's sovereign will. He is responsible for his choices.

When reduced to its simplest elements election is twofold. First, God elected a plan of salvation which he accomplished in Christ. Man may either reject this plan or accept it. Romans 8:29–30 means that an omniscient God knew beforehand who would reject or accept his salvation. But his foreknowledge does not make him responsible for man's choice. God proposes to justify, or declare righteous, all who accept his plan. He will glorify all such in the end.

Second, God elected a people to make known his elected plan of salvation (cf. Gen. 12:2–3; Ex. 19:5–6; Matt. 21:33–41; 1 Pet. 2:4–10). Salvation is not merely a privilege to be enjoyed. It is a gospel to be shared. To refuse to do so does not deprive a Christian of his salvation, but he loses the privilege of being used in God's glorious redemptive purpose.

Thus election is to both salvation and evangelism. In both the free will of man determines the final result. By free will men can elect to be saved but elect to be barren Christians. God forbid! Men can also elect to be both saved and fruitful Christians. In such lives the sovereign will of God and the free will of man find their divinely intended relationship (John 15:16).

8
Last Things

Our Christian faith emphasizes the future. The past is important, for Christ's "once for all" atonement is a past event. The present likewise is important, for it is the time of decision and Christian living. Both past and present, however, can be seen in true perspective only by remembering what the Bible teaches us about the future. The God who has acted in the past, and is acting even now, will continue to act. Our faith rests in the confidence that the future is in his hands.

Death

In the New Testament the word for "death" is used in three ways: (1) the death of the body wherein the soul is separated from the body (John 11:4; Acts 2:24; Phil. 2:27,30); (2) the misery of the soul which results from the separation of the soul from God by sin, beginning on earth but continuing after death (Rom. 7:13; 2 Cor. 3:7; Eph. 2:1); (3) the final state of the wicked in hell (Rom. 1:32; Rev. 20:14; 21:8). All three are the result of sin (1 Cor. 15:21–22,56).

The New Testament does not regard physical death for the righteous with the dread found in the Old Testament. Jesus called the physical death of Lazarus "sleep" (John 11:11–14).

Paul said, "For to me to live is Christ, and to die is gain" (Phil. 1:21 ff.). Even so, death is regarded as an enemy (1 Cor. 15:26), one which God makes to serve him, nevertheless, in releasing the Christian from a mortal body to receive an immortal one at the resurrection (Rom. 7:24–25; 1 Cor. 15:50 ff.).

The greater emphasis in the New Testament is placed upon spiritual death. Even while men are alive physically, they may be dead spiritually (Eph. 2:1 ff.; cf. Luke 15:24). The soul that is separated from God by sin is dead, though actually the soul is immortal (John 5:24; 6:50; 8:21). But those who are alive spiritually shall never die spiritually (John 11:25–26). Thus for these physical death is shorn of its terror (1 Cor. 15:55–57).

The intermediate state is the period between physical death and the resurrection. At death the physical body returns to the earth. But the souls of both the righteous and unrighteous enter Hades, the abode of the dead. Jesus entered Hades (Acts 2:31), as did the rich man in the parable (Luke 16:23). The rich man and Lazarus were in Hades but separated, the former in torment and the latter in bliss (Luke 16:25). Unfortunately "Hades" is translated "hell" in the King James Version (1 Cor. 15:55, "grave"). But the Greek had a different word for the place of punishment (*Gehenna*). The English context, however, makes the distinction quite clear.

At physical death, therefore, all enter Hades and remain in a conscious state. The lost endure punishment; the saved enjoy fellowship with Christ (cf. Luke 16). At the judgment this state of each is fixed eternally. There is no scriptural basis for "soul sleeping." "Hades" is never used in the sense of purgatory. No such idea is taught in the New Testament.

Resurrection

The fact of the resurrection is taught in the Old Testament (Isa. 26:19; Ezek. 37:1–14; Dan. 12:2), but it is more clearly seen in the New Testament (Matt. 22:23–33; John 5:25–29; 11:23 ff.; Rom. 1:4; 8:11; 1 Cor. 15). The New Testament bases man's resurrection on that of Jesus (1 Cor. 15:12 ff.).

The word "resurrection" renders a Greek word meaning to stand again. It means something dead which is made alive again. Thus, resurrection refers not merely to spiritual immortality but to a bodily resurrection from the dead. Jesus rose bodily from the dead. He was seen alive after his burial, the word "see" rendering a word meaning to see with the natural eye. Thus the postresurrection appearances of Jesus were not mere visions, but they were actual bodily appearances viewed by physical sight.

What of the resurrection body? Paul in 1 Corinthians 15 says that it will be as different from the natural body as the harvest from the seed (vv. 36–38). It will exceed the natural body in glory as celestial bodies exceed terrestrial (vv. 40–42). It will be a body adapted to the heavenly life as natural bodies are adapted to their natural habitat (v. 39). It will be incorruptible (vv. 42 ff.) and not subject to pain or death (Rev. 21:4).

Jesus' resurrection body was similar to the one he had in life. His disciples recognized him. Yet, it was different. His body was not subject to the laws of time, space, or thickness (Matt. 28:2 ff.; Luke 24:15–31,34; John 20:19). So will be the resurrection body of the Christian. "We know that, when he shall appear, we shall be like him" (1 John 3:2).

Those Christians who are alive at Christ's second coming shall be changed immediately (1 Cor. 15:51 ff.). But their translation into heaven will be preceded by the bodily resurrection of those who lie in the cemetery (1 Thess. 4:15–18). God will bring the souls of the righteous dead with him to be united with their resurrection bodies (1 Thess. 4:14). All will be caught up to meet the Lord in the air. "And so shall we ever be with the Lord" (1 Thess. 4:17).

The righteous dead will be raised unto life everlasting. The unrighteous dead will be cast into hell, which is the second death (Rev. 20:14-15).

Second Coming of Christ

The second coming of Christ is the "blessed hope" of the Christian (Titus 2:13). Varying positions may be held as to the detailed events accompanying the end of the age, but the fact of our Lord's return is abundantly and clearly taught in the New Testament (Matt. 13:24-30,36-43,47-50; 16:27; 24:3-51; 1 Cor. 1:7-8; 1 Thess. 4:13-18; Heb. 9:28). In the first century, as well as today, many doubted his return (2 Peter 3:1-13), but "the Lord is not slack concerning his promise" (v. 9).

Jesus taught much about his second coming. Negatively, he warned against false signs of his appearance (Matt. 24:4), false messiahs (vv. 5,24), wars and rumors of wars (v. 6), famines, earthquakes, and pestilences (v. 7). The import is that men will mistake normal happenings of history as signs of his return. We are not to be deceived thereby. Life will go its normal way, until without warning he will appear (vv. 37-39).

Positively, Jesus taught that his return is an assured fact (Matt. 16:27; 24:44). The time of Christ's coming is unrevealed (24:36). When conditions are right he will come (v. 28). Only one certain sign did Jesus give, and this refers to condition, not to time (v. 14). The time is hidden in the mind of the Father (v. 36).

But his coming will be outward, visible, and personal (Acts 1:11). The attitude of the Christian should be one of constant expectancy (Matt. 24:44). Jesus' coming is described as like that of a thief (24:43; 1 Thess. 5:2,4). At a time when you least expect him, he will come. The early Christians lived in daily expectancy of the Lord's return (1 Thess. 4:17). Some will be alive at his return. Each generation should regard itself as that one (1 Cor. 15:15 ff.).

At the Lord's return there will be the resurrection of the dead and the transformation of the living (1 Thess. 4:13–18). Here Paul is thinking of those who are in Christ. The important thing is to be ready for his coming. The details we can leave with him. (Hobbs, *Fundamentals of our Faith,* chap. 13).

Millennium

The word "millennium" does not appear in the English Bible. It is a term in theology used of the "thousand years" mentioned in Revelation 20:2–7. It is of Latin derivation—*milli anni,* "thousand years." This is a translation of the Greek, *chilia etē,* meaning the same thing.

References to a millennium are found in Jewish apocalyptic literature (cf. Slavonic Enoch, chapters 32–33). Mention of it is also found in the Talmud. Some trace the idea back to Babylonia or Persia.

The New Testament reference to this doctrine, sometimes called chiliasm, is confined to the passage in Revelation, although by some it is related in interpretation to other New Testament teachings regarding eschatology or the doctrine of last things. Beginning in the second century A.D. the doctrine is found in certain noncanonical writings.

There are three general views with regard to the millennium. Postmillennialism believes that after a thousand years of peace and righteousness, made possible by the gospel, Christ will return with one general resurrection and judgment, followed by the eternal reign of Christ. Premillennialism holds that Christ will return before the thousand years. It sees two resurrections and two or more judgments, followed by Christ's eternal reign. There are varying positions within this group, some of which deal with minute details of events. A-millennialism regards the thousand years as figurative. The word "a-millennium" means "no millennium" or that the thousand years are not to be taken literally (cf. 2 Peter 3:8). To this group the return of Christ will be attended by one general resurrection and judgment which will terminate history and inaugurate Christ's eternal reign. Within this group one position (e.g. Augustine) regards the millennium as the entire Christian era which terminates with Christ's return. Another (e.g. Kliefoth) holds the millennium to be the eternal, heavenly state itself.

Baptists generally hold to the premillennial or the a-millennial position. One's position on this has never been a test of faith or fellowship among them. Generally, they agree on the facts of Christ's return, the resurrection and judgment, and Christ's eternal reign. They hold to "unity in diversity" as to the details.

Judgment

The principle of judgment is found throughout the Scriptures (Isa. 42:1,3–4; Matt. 10:15; 24; Heb. 9:27; 2 Pet. 2:4,9; Rev. 14:7), which teach also a final judgment (Matt. 25:31 ff.; Rev. 20:11 ff.). In the final judgment Christ will be the Judge (Matt. 19:2–8; 25:31–46; Rev. 3:21; 20:11–12).

In 2 Corinthians 5:10, Paul says, "We must all appear before the judgment seat of Christ; that every one may receive the things done in his body, according to that he hath done, whether it be good or bad." The picture of the judgment in Revelation 20:11–15 is most revealing. There the dead, small and great, stand before God. The "books . . . and another book . . . which is the book of life" are opened. The dead are judged by those things "written in the books, according to their works." Those whose names are written in the "book of life" have already been judged in Christ as to their redemption. Thus they are saved from hell. Those whose names are not written in the book of life shall be cast into hell. All men shall be judged, not to determine character, but to reveal or declare it. From the "books" will be declared the degrees of reward in heaven for the saved and the degrees of punishment in hell for the lost.

Students of the New Testament differ as to whether there is one judgment or multiple judgments. This writer sees one general judgment with the various accounts giving different aspects to it. Many sincere scholars disagree with this position. This matter is not a test of fellowship or orthodoxy. The fact of a final judgment is sure. The details we can leave to the Lord.

But one thing is clear. All men shall appear for judgment before the great white throne (Rev. 20:11-15). The ones saved by grace will be glorified and rewarded according to their works and will enter into the indescribable bliss of eternal heaven (Rev. 21-22). The lost will be doomed and punished according to their works in the indescribable anguish of eternal hell (Rev. 20:15).

Today Christ is the Saviour. Then he will be the Judge. His judgment will be one of love. To the saved it will be that of a love received; to the lost it will be that of a love rejected.

Heaven

The Greek word for heaven (*ouranos*) carried three meanings: the aerial heavens where clouds and birds are (Luke 4:25; 9:54), the starry heavens (Mark 13:25), and the highest heaven where God dwells (Matt. 5:34; Rev. 4:1). Bible teachings about heaven in this last sense are restrained. They exhaust language in describing its glory (1 Cor. 2:9). Since the language is largely symbolic, the reality must be greater than the symbol.

Heaven is a place (John 14:2), but the Bible does not locate it. However, it is where God and Christ are, and that will be heaven enough. It is a place of glory. Gold and precious stones (Rev. 21:18 ff.) suggest moral values; white robes (Rev. 6:11) imply purity; there will be leaves for healing (Rev. 22:2) and crowns for victory (Rev. 4:10). The "unclean" will not be there (Rev. 21:27).

Heaven will be relief (Rev. 21:4,12–13). It is reward. Rewards will be in degree to the Christian's service on earth (Matt. 25:14–30; Luke 19:12–17). Some will be saved "as by fire" (1 Cor. 3:14–15). The soul will be saved, but useless works will be burned. To all the saved is promised victory over Satan.

Heaven will also mean realization. The "white stone" (Rev. 2:17) probably means fulness of personality. It involves complete knowledge (1 Cor. 13:8–12), ideal service (Rev. 22:3–4) and worship (21:22), perfect fellowship with God (Heb. 12:22–23; Rev. 7:4–11), holiness of character (Rev. 3:5; 21:27), fulness of life (Matt. 25:46), and fellowship with Christ (John 14:3; Rev. 3:21).

Heaven will mean appreciation (Rev. 15:3). There Christ will receive praise and honor (4:10–11; 5:9–12). Heaven will mean endless growth (1 Cor. 13:12; Eph. 3:18–19). With the hindrances of the flesh removed, we shall go on growing in grace and knowledge of Christ in an endless eternity.

Comparing Genesis 2:8–25 and Revelation 22:1–5, it appears that heaven will embody the restoration of the conditions of Eden.

Hell

The New Testament word translated "hell," denoting a place of punishment, is *Gehenna*. It refers to the vale of Hinnom, a valley located south and east of Jerusalem (Josh. 15:8, Matt. 5:22,29–30; 10:28; 18:9; 23:15,33; Mark 9:43,45,47; Luke 12:5; James 3:6). In the Old Testament it was a place of human sacrifice to the pagan fire-god, Molech (2 Kings 23:10). Its practice was abolished by Josiah. The place was so abhorred by the Jews that they made it a garbage dump. Into it they cast the refuse of Jerusalem, including dead animals and the unclaimed bodies of executed criminals. To consume the garbage, fires burned day and night. Maggots worked constantly, and wild dogs howled and fought over the bodies.

Jesus adopted this horrible scene to depict hell. In this light his words take on terrible imagery (Matt. 8:12; 13:42; 22:13; 25:30; Mark 9:43–44).

Thus we have the gruesome picture of hell. Revelation 20:10,14–15 pictures it as a lake of fire. Into it will be cast the devil and his angels (Matt. 25:41) and all whose names are not written in the book of life. This is called the second death or the eternal separation of lost souls from God. While the location is not given in the Bible, hell is a place as heaven is a place.

Some insist that hell is not fire. If not, it is something infinitely worse than fire. The Bible employs language picturing the greatest suffering to describe it. No wonder that Jesus warned against it and paid such a price to save men from it! Of interest is the fact that every reference to *Gehenna* as a place of punishment fell from the lips of Jesus. Infinite Love is warning us against infinite suffering and horror.

There will be degrees of punishment in hell as there are degrees of reward in heaven (Luke 12:47–48). There will be greater punishment for one who sins against a knowledge of Christ (Matt. 11:21–24) than for the ignorant savage who never heard of him. But both will be there (Rom. 2:6,12,15; 4:15). As there will be eternal life in heaven, so will there be eternal torment in hell (Matt. 25:46). The Bible does not teach soul annihilation.

Many people deny the existence of hell. Yet Jesus said more about hell than he did about heaven. Such denial is due more to wishful thinking and sentimental reasoning than to an interpretation of the factual teaching of the Bible. To say that a merciful God would not make a hell is to examine only one facet of God's nature. He is love. But he is holiness and right-eousness also. God sends no one to hell. Each person goes there of his own will despite all that God in Christ has done to prevent it.

Kingdom

The "kingdom" is not to be equated with the "church." Ac-tually in the larger sense, the "kingdom of God" is the rule of God in his universe and over all created beings, of which the church is a spiritual element. Kingdom means sovereignty. Some would distinguish between the "kingdom of God" and the "kingdom of heaven." But an analysis reveals that the various gospels record these terms as interchangeable within the same teaching of Jesus (cf. Mark 4:30–32 and Matt. 13:31–32).

In its [kingdom] final state God will reign over a redeemed creation (Rom. 8:19–22; 2 Peter 3:13, Rev. 21:1); over Satan, his angels, and the unregenerate in hell (1 Cor. 15:24–28; Phil. 2:10–11; Rev. 20:10–15); and in heaven over the holy angels and the redeemed of all ages (Rev. 21–22).

When Jesus came he did so to establish God's reign, not only in men's hearts, but over all things in the universe. Each time a soul submits to Christ he willingly submits to God's rule. As such he becomes a part of the church general. But in the end all, either willingly or unwillingly, will acknowledge Jesus as Lord and Christ to the glory of God the Father (Phil. 2:10–11). This does not mean universal salvation. The saved will have submitted to God by faith prior to Jesus' second coming. The lost will be submitted to an acknowledgement of God's rule by force, the force of God's will, at the final judgment.

The nature of the final state of the kingdom is seen in 1 Corin-thians 15:24–28. Jesus is reigning now in his mediatorial king-dom (vv. 25–26). The condition will come when he shall have subdued the entire universe, material and spiritual, unto himself. It will be completed at the judgment. Then the kingdom will be delivered up to the Father, that God may be all in all (v. 28).

Note in this passage the presence of the Trinity: God the Father and God the Son by name, and God the Holy Spirit by the implication of revelation in the Scriptures. "That God may be all in all" does not mean that the Son and Holy Spirit will cease to be. It means that Father, Son, and Holy Spirit are God in his triune revelation. It means further that the ultimate reign of God in his triune nature will be absolute.

9
Miscellany

Preceding chapters have dealt with central subject areas of Christian doctrine, but many facets of belief have not been mentioned. The present chapter brings some of the more important ones into view. It looks first at some vital points in the relationship between Christians and civil government. It then moves to three topics of wide interest—angels, Satan, and the virgin Mary.

Civil Government

The New Testament teaches that the institution of government is ordained of God (Rom. 13:1b). The word "ordained" indicates a fixed purpose of God. This does not refer to any particular government or form of government. Nor does it teach the "divine right of kings." It simply means that God has ordained civil government as a means of peaceful and orderly living. Thus every man is to submit to constituted government (v. 1a). Lawlessness is rebellion against the will of God, for which wrongdoers shall receive judgment ("damnation" is *krima*, judgment) at the hands of the state. Law abiding citizens should regard rulers as constituted for their good rather than harm (v. 3).

Paul calls the one in authority a "minister [*diakonos*, servant, word for deacon] of God to thee for good" (v. 4). He also calls him a "minister [*leitourgos*] of God" or "God's ministers" (v. 6). *Leitourgos* means a public minister or servant of the state. It is also used of temple priests who render a religious service. Thus the ruler, like the priest, renders a divinely ordained service (Vincent). Government, therefore, is elevated to the religious sphere. This does not mean that God approves of a given ruler. Nero, a bestial pagan, was the Roman emperor when Paul wrote these words. He has in mind the office not the person. During the same period Peter wrote, "Honour the king" (1 Peter 2:17)—the office, not necessarily the man.

The ruler "beareth not the sword in vain." He is "a revenger to execute wrath upon him that doeth evil" (Rom. 13:4). The "sword" referred to the ruler's power and right to inflict capital punishment.

The Christian citizen is to obey law, not from fear, but for conscience's sake (v. 5). He pays taxes as a part of his responsibility under a constituted government (vv. 6–7). "Tribute" (*phoros*) is that which is paid by a subject people to a subjecting nation (Luke 20:22). "Custom" (*telos*) is the tax paid for the support of civil government (Matt. 17:25).

In this passage Paul takes no account of the right of revolt against tyranny. He assumes righteous government. The New Testament teaches that no government has the right to expect men to disobey God (Acts 4:19–20). But legitimate procedures of repeal of unjust laws, not disobedience of law, should be the route followed. Common sense teaches that revolt should come only after all reasonable means of redress have failed or when a given government is so in revolt against God's purpose as to forfeit its right to exist. History records that the Christian faith has lived under all types of civil government, both good and evil.

Christian Citizenship

Every Christian is related to the constituted government under which he lives (Rom. 13:1–7). And a good Christian will be a good citizen (vv. 5 ff.). Paul prided himself in his Roman citizenship and availed himself of the protection granted thereby (Acts 22:25–29; cf. 21:39). Jesus, a member of a subjected people, obeyed the laws of Rome where they did not conflict with the law of God (Luke 23:4,14; John 18:38; 19:4,6). Note that there was no incident of conflict. He repeatedly refused to lead in a rebellion against the Empire (Matt. 4:8–10; 26:52–53; John 6:15; Acts 1:6–7). He recognized the dual obligation which the Christian holds toward the State and God (Matt. 22:17 ff.). Though his first allegiance was to his Father, yet he recognized the right of government (temple) to levy taxes and submitted to it (17:24 ff.).

The Christian citizen is to be in the world but not of it (John 17:14 ff.; 1 Cor. 5:9–10). He is to change society not by violence but by influence and witness (Matt. 5:13–16). For instance, Jesus never made an open onslaught against slavery. Certainly he did not approve it. Yet his principles and example broke the shackles of bondage and sounded the death knell to any attitude or institution which degrades men (cf. Matt. 12:11–12; 16:26; see also Philemon). Satan offered Jesus a short cut to an ideal society, but he chose the way of the cross (Matt. 4:9–10). He sought to change society by regeneration, not revolution (Matt. 16:24–25; John 3:5). Changed men should seek to change abuses in society by Christian means (Rom. 6:12 ff.; Eph. 5:1–18).

Men are not saved by social reform (Rom. 10:3), yet the gospel has its social aspects (cf. Epistle of James; see also Matt. 5:13–14; 7:24 ff.; 25:31 ff.). The Christian is to go beyond the legal demands to Christian conduct (Matt. 5:20 ff.). He is to be motivated by a Christian conscience (Rom. 13:5) and love (1 Cor. 13). He should settle his differences within Christian principles, not legal procedures (6:1–8). He should renounce personal rights for his Christian witness (1 Cor. 8). In all relations of life he should be Christian in his conduct (Eph. 5:22–6:9; Col. 3:1 to 4:6).

The Christian's first citizenship is in the kingdom of God (Matt. 5–7). The Philippian church is called "a colony of heaven" (Phil. 3:20, Moffatt). Philippi was a Roman colony, enjoying certain privileges but bearing corresponding responsibilities. It was a little bit of Rome in a subjected area, whose manner of life was to create a desire in the conquered people to be Romans. As "a colony of heaven" Christians should so live as to change a pagan society and by their manner of life to witness to the saving power of the gospel. Thus a genuine Christian citizenship is evangelism in shoes (Matt. 5:16).

Separation of Church and State

The Pharisees and Herodians faced Jesus with a loaded question (Matt. 22:15–17). Involved was their messianic concept which forbade payment of taxes to a pagan power. To answer categorically either way would have involved Jesus in trouble with the Romans or the Jews. Jesus did neither (Matt. 22:18). The coin testified to the Jews' subservience to and dependence upon the State (vv. 19–20). They also recognized their relationship toward God. Jesus pointed out their obligations to both God and the State (v. 21). Thus we have the basic text on separation of church and state.

The principle of the separation of church and state does not mean that the two have no relations whatever. Jesus recognized the existence, rights, and functions of the State (Matt. 22:15–21). The early Christians in missionary work utilized roads and sea lanes provided by the State (cf. Paul's travels, Acts 13–16; 27). On occasion Paul accepted or called for the protection of the State (Acts 18:12 ff.; 21:27 ff.; 22:25 ff.; 25:10–12). At the same time Christians were exhorted to submit to the authority of the State (Rom. 13:1 ff.; 1 Peter 2:12–17). Even when persecuted by the State they were to endure it willingly as a testimony unto the Lord (1 Peter 3:14–15). In the peaceful existence of an orderly society they were to carry on their spiritual work (1 Tim. 2:1 ff.).

Church and state are mutually related in the normal events of life. The state provides a proper atmosphere in which the churches carry on their work (cf. fire and police protection, national security, postal service, and general stability in society). In turn the churches endeavor to produce through the gospel the type of Christian character conducive to a well-ordered society.

But church and state are also mutually exclusive. Neither shall endeavor to control the other or to use it in the discharge of its separate responsibility. The church shall not seek to achieve its spiritual goals through political power (cf. Matt. 4:8–10; John 6:15). Nor shall the state commandeer the church for political ends (Acts 4:19). No religion shall be favored above another. The state shall not levy taxes upon strictly religious property, nor shall any church receive tax funds to be used in the performance of its spiritual, educational, and healing ministry (cf. 1 Cor. 16:1 ff.). The church shall be free to determine its own form of worship, faith, government, membership, and missionary outreach. But such shall be carried on within the framework of the laws of the state.

Various religious groups are not agreed on the distinct line of demarcation in the separation of church and state. Obviously there are "gray" areas which account for these differences. Baptists may differ as to the line but not the principle. They have always been its leading champions. The greatest progress in Baptist witness in history has come under this principle.

Religious Liberty

Religious liberty is the mother of all true liberty. It is based upon the dignity of each individual made in the "image of God" (Gen. 1:27) and his competency to stand before God without the mediation of earthly priest or king (1 Tim. 2:1–6). It is not a privilege granted by man but a right given of God. It recognizes the supreme worth of each individual soul (Matt. 16:26). And it demands that each man shall be free to worship God according to the dictates of his own heart. Religious freedom is more than freedom from outward coercion. It is freedom for inward determination. Religion must be free to practice and propagate its beliefs. And men must be free to receive or reject them. God made man free, but he also made him responsible for his choices. But the choices must be his own.

Religious liberty in the Christian sense involves the absolute lordship of Jesus Christ (Rom. 10:9, RSV, "confess . . . Jesus is Lord"). True liberty is found only in him (John 8:36; cf. Rom. 8:1–2). It is exercised under the guidance and power of the Holy Spirit (Rom. 8:5–6; 2 Cor. 3:17). And this lordship supersedes all other authority (Acts 4:19–20; 5:29).

Religious liberty does not mean license (Gal. 5:13; 2 Peter 2:19 ff.). For liberty involves responsibility. Freedom without responsibility is not freedom but anarchy. Religious liberty demands inner and personal controls (Rom. 6:6–18).

The doctrine of religious liberty does not stem from any legal document of a political state. It is rooted in the teachings of the Bible. And if the Bible be forsaken or relegated to a place of nonimportance, religious liberty will not long endure. A free state does not create religious freedom. But religious freedom alone can make a state truly free.

Baptists are not the only champions of religious freedom. But history records them among the forefront of the struggle for religious freedom. Both in England and America they were among the first and most consistent advocates of full religious liberty. They can claim a large share in the establishment of the American principle of complete separation of church and state—a principle that continues to need our support.

Angels

Some insist that belief in angels is merely a residue from heathen and primitive beliefs, since such beliefs were held by all ancient peoples. But universality of belief does not mean a false concept. We cannot assume that God did not create other intelligent beings besides man.

The Bible clearly teaches the existence of angels as created beings (Psalm 148:2-5). In the Bible angels appear in human form (Gen. 18:2; 19:13) but in other ways also (Matt. 1:20; Luke 2:13; 1 Cor. 6:3). The word "angel" (Hebrew, *malak*; Greek, *angelos*) means "messenger." Angels are God's messengers to do his work and will (Heb. 1:14). The "angel of the covenant" or "angel of the Lord" is usually identified with God or the Second Person of the Trinity (Gen. 31:13; 32:30; Judges 2:1-5; 6:11).

The "angels of the seven churches" of Asia Minor are usually regarded as their pastors (Rev. 1:20). Jesus speaks of the angels of little children, or those who believe on him, as being before the Father in heaven (Matt. 18:10). Are these guardian angels?

The Bible forbids the worshiping of angels (Col. 2:18). Instead it teaches that the saints shall judge the angels (1 Cor. 6:3).

The Bible speaks of fallen angels. Angels were created as holy beings, since a holy God could create no other. But Jude speaks of "angels which kept not their first estate" (v. 6). Peter refers to "angels that sinned" and were cast down to hell, bound in "chains of darkness, to be reserved unto judgment" (2 Peter 2:4). Pride seems to be the cause of their fall (1 Tim. 3:6).

The chief fallen angel is Satan. With the fallen angels he shall be cast into the lake of fire. All lost sinners as children of their father, the devil, will be cast into the lake of fire prepared for the devil and his angels (Matt. 25:41).

Satan

"Satan" is one of several names given in the Bible for the personal being who is the source of all evil. It means "adversary." He is also called "devil" or "slanderer" (Matt. 4:1), Abaddon and Apollyon (destroyer, Rev. 9:11), Beelzebub (Matt. 12:24), Belial (2 Cor. 6:15), prince of devils (Matt. 12:24), prince of the power of the air (Eph. 2:2), prince of this world (John 14:30), and Lucifer, son of the morning (Isa. 14:12). From this last reference it would seem that he is a fallen angel, cast out of heaven because he rebelled against God (cf. 2 Peter 2:4; Jude 6).

Significant is the fact that while in the Scriptures Satan always appears before God in his true light (cf. Job 1:6 ff.; Matt. 4:3 ff.), he never appears to man as such (cf. Gen. 3:1 ff., "serpent" here probably a graceful, beautiful creature). Paul says that he often appears to man as an "angel of light" (2 Cor. 11:14). God knows him for who he is; man is deceived by him. The Bible pictures him in his true light as "your adversary the devil, as a roaring lion, walketh about, seeking whom he may devour" (1 Peter 5:8).

As the slanderer, the devil slanders God to man (Gen. 3:1-5) and man to God (Job 1:9 ff.). As the adversary or Satan, he successfully tempts man to rebel against God. He even stormed the bastion of the character of Jesus only to fail (Matt. 4:1-11; Luke 4:1-13). Satan is a power second only to God but is subject to God (Job 1:6). God permits him to go so far but prescribes a limit beyond which he shall not go

(Job 1:12; 2:6). In his opposition to God he perverts the Scriptures (Matt. 4:6), opposes God's work (1 Thess. 2:18), hinders the gospel (2 Cor. 4:4), works lying wonders (Rev. 16:14), and is the father of lies (John 8:44).

Jesus Christ was manifested to destroy the works of the devil (1 John 3:8). Satan's dethronement which began in the ministry of Jesus (Luke 10:18), and was accomplished in his death and resurrection (Col. 2:15), will be culminated when the devil and his angels will be cast into the lake of fire (Rev. 20:10).

Virgin Mary

Other than tradition and the apocryphal gospels (not Scripture), nothing is known about the virgin Mary apart from the record of the New Testament. "Mary" is the Greek form of the Hebrew word "Miriam" (cf. Ex. 15:20). She was a member of the tribe of Judah (Luke 3:30). As a peasant girl she lived in Nazareth (1:26–27), although she traced her lineage back to Bethlehem through David (2:4, with Joseph). She was a cousin of Elizabeth, the mother of John the Baptist (1:36).

As a young maiden, probably about sixteen (the apocryphal gospels say twelve), she was betrothed to Joseph a carpenter, a man probably much older than Mary (Matt. 1:18). In Jewish life betrothal was more than our engagement but was not equal to our marriage. By her own admission her character is unassailable (Luke 1:34).

As a virgin she received God's revelation that she was to bear his Son (Matt. 1:18; Luke 1:26 ff.). She was a woman of great faith and submission (Luke 1:38,46 ff.) but not one without wonder. The first question as to the possibility of the virgin Birth came from Mary (Luke 1:34).

After the birth of Jesus, Mary entered into the normal relations of married life. She and Joseph became the parents of four sons and at least two daughters (Matt. 13:55–56). Roman and Greek Catholics, holding to the perpetual virginity of Mary, see these as "cousins" of Jesus, or else children of Joseph by a former marriage. But the more natural meaning of the text is that they were half-brothers and half-sisters of Jesus by Mary and Joseph.

The New Testament does not record where Jesus ever referred directly to Mary as "mother," although he doubtless regarded her as such. But the New Testament does make such references. In his public ministry Jesus referred to a higher relationship (Matt. 12:46 ff.). His references to Mary as "woman" (John 2:4; 19:26) were not terms of disrespect. When properly understood they carried the highest respect.

The "sword" truly pierced through Mary's soul (Luke 2:35) as she followed Jesus to his cross (John 19:25). There Jesus showed his tender care for her as he committed her to his beloved disciple (John 19:26–27). She is listed among the group in the upper room after Jesus' ascension (Acts 1:14). Tradition says that she lived with John until her death in old age, probably at Ephesus.

Mary should be reverenced as one highly favored of God (Luke 1:30) and the mother of our Saviour. But the New Testament does not justify the extravagant claims made for her by the Roman Catholic Church.